LIVING DANGER- OUSLY

"Some dead men will read
these pages. That does not mean that they
are peculiar people. Actually they are
~~~ ordinary, for the world has a large

S E

LIVING DANGEROUSLY

Copyright © 1968 by
Zondervan Publishing House,
Grand Rapids, Michigan.

Library of Congress Catalog Card Number: 68-55322

The Scripture Text preceding Chapter 4 is taken from *The Amplified Bible* and is used by permission.

First printing		1968
Second printing		1969
Third printing		1970
Fourth printing	January	1971
Fifth printing	July	1971
Sixth printing	January	1972
Seventh printing	Nov.	1972

Printed in the United States of America

Contents

Chapter 1

Jesus therefore again groaning in himself cometh to the grave. It was a cave, and a stone lay upon it.

Jesus said, Take ye away the stone. Martha, the sister of him that was dead, saith unto him, Lord, by this time he stinketh: for he hath been dead four days.

Jesus saith unto her, Said I not unto thee, that, if thou wouldest believe, thou shouldest see the glory of God?

Then they took away the stone from the place where the dead was laid. And Jesus lifted up his eyes, and said, Father, I thank thee that thou hast heard me.

And I knew that thou hearest me always: but because of the people which stand by I said it, that they may believe that thou hast sent me.

And when he thus had spoken, he cried with a loud voice, Lazarus, come forth.

And he that was dead came forth, bound hand and foot with graveclothes: and his face was bound about with a napkin. Jesus saith unto them, Loose him, and let him go.

John 11:38-44

1

The Return of a Dead Man

LAZARUS WAS DEAD. THERE WAS ONLY ONE THING WRONG WITH him, but as a result there was not one thing right with him! Popularity does not count much when a man is dead. A girl's good looks are irrelevant when she dies. In fact all things that people think are so important, such as wealth and happiness, suddenly lose their attraction when death stalks in.

There is only one thing wrong with many people in the world today. They are dead. Some dead men will read these pages. That does not mean that they are peculiar people. Actually, they are very ordinary, for the world has a large population of dead people. It is by no means uncommon to see dead men eating and drinking, laughing and crying. They are all around us. You may be dead as you read these pages!

Let me explain. When we talk about death we automatically think in terms of bodies and funerals and graves. This is physical death, but this is not the only kind of death. Human beings are not bodies only, and therefore they cannot be explained and understood purely in physical terms.

Have you ever heard someone say, "I have just lost my father"? They meant that their father had died. But they had not really lost their father, because he was lying perfectly still where they had left him. Of course they knew that what was lying there was not their father at all. It was only his shell. They have lost him, but his shell remains. In the same way people sometimes say, "Mother has passed away." Then they add, "Would you like to see her?" This is rather bewildering. If mother has gone how can we see her? If we can see her why say that she has passed away? The answer is that the real person has gone, and in the process of going has vacated the old house, or the shell that we call the body.

This "person" that leaves the body at death is called the soul. Everyone who has a body has a soul. You would not always get that impression, but it is true. The soul can think, decide and desire. It can know and love, hate and react. In short, it could be defined as the personality.

Animals have personalities. They are not just bodies, in fact, you could almost say that they are personalities living in bodies. But no self-respecting human being either thinks of himself or allows anyone else to think of him as an animal! If we want to insult people we usually call them some kind of animal. "You eat like a pig," or "He hasn't got the brains of a gnat," or even "She has the morals of an alleycat!" To call a human being an animal is the deadliest of insults. But if man and animals are so similar, why does man get offended if he is called an animal? If an animal has a body and a personality similar to a human being, why do human beings consider themselves so superior?

Many people say that a man is superior to an animal because he is more highly developed. But it isn't altogether true to say that man's superiority over the animals stems solely from a more sophisticated development of his body and personality. Man's superiority is a result of his possessing something in addition to his body and soul that an animal does not possess. This something is called the *spirit*.

It is man's spirit that is so important. His body enables him to be conscious of the physical aspects of life. He eats and he breathes, he runs and he sleeps and he sees. All this he does with his body. His body enables him to see people, to walk toward them, to hear what they say, and to shake them by the hand. But his body can never enable him to make a friend of the person whom he has seen, with whom he has talked or whose hand he has shaken. It is his soul that enables him to do this, for his soul enables him to understand the person, to respond to the person or to react against him. His soul even gives him the capacity to love the person and so the soul is that part of him that enables him to have a deeper relationship than a purely physical one. He can enjoy the person that he has recognized physically in a social way too, because he is blessed with a soul.

But the spirit is absolutely unique. It gives man a re-markable capacity. This capacity can be defined as the ability to know and to enjoy God. It is this ability that makes man superior. The spirit of a man makes even the lowest man far superior to the highest animal.

No one has ever seen an animal with a sense of God. You have never seen a cow standing on its hind legs praying! But strange as it may seem in these days of agnosticism and atheism every human being has some inherent sense of the reality of God. I believe that no one is born an atheist, and that the only people who profess to be atheists or agnostics are those people who at some time have decided to reject the things concerning God that are inherent in the depth of their beings. It is a remarkable thing that so many people who deny the existence of God, such as atheists, or discount or disregard His existence such as many agnostics, are so enthusiastic in their arguments against Him. They appear to take this Person, whom they say does not exist, very seriously! I believe that one of the reasons they take Him so seriously is simply that they have an inherent consciousness and awareness of His existence.

In addition to this it is true to say that there never was a human being who did not have a god of some kind. There is something inside a man that makes him long for something or someone bigger than himself for whom he can live, and upon whom he can depend, or around which his life can revolve. His god may be an ambition or a hobby, a person, or even himself, but somewhere he will have a god. Man is made like this. He is incapable of being without a god. Even the most primitive tribes ever known to man betray evidences of this. Tribes that live in the most remote corners of the earth have invariably been found to have their own private gods whom they either fear, or respect, or worship, or serve. At the other end of the scale even the most sophisticated *échelons* of society demonstrate man's ability and capacity to know a god of some kind. Yes, even though man may wish to deny it or discount it, he has within himself a certain knowledge of God and a certain capacity to know God.

So far we have seen that man operates on three planes. Physically with his body, socially with his soul, and spiritually with his spirit. It follows quite obviously that if it is possible for him to operate on three planes it is also possible that he may not necessarily operate on all three planes simultaneously. For instance, if his body stops operating he will be physically dead, but that does not automatically mean that he will be spiritually dead. Or because his body is going along fine does not mean that his spirit is functioning perfectly.

Therefore it is possible to be physically alive but spiritually dead in one and the same moment. If you are reading this you are most certainly physically alive! But do not assume that you are necessarily spiritually alive, for it is quite possible that you could be reading this and be dead.

This is not a figment of my imagination. The Bible says, "She that liveth in pleasure is dead while she liveth" (I Timothy 5:6). It also tells about people who were alive enough to read a letter that was written to them in the church at Ephesus which described them as being alive after being dead.

Jesus also startled some men by saying, "I am come that they might have life" (John 10:10) but they were physically alive! So obviously He had not come to give physical men who were physically alive more physical life.

The lady mentioned by Paul and the Christians in Ephesus had not died physically. No, they were very much physically alive, but they were spiritually dead. They needed the life that Jesus talked about.

Would you like to know if you are dead? It is a simple thing to find out. Dead men have no appetite. When Lazarus was alive he got hungry regularly, but once he died he lost all interest in the food that his sisters prepared. No matter how appetizing the food was, how delicious were the aromas that came from their kitchen he was totally unmoved. One of the symptoms of spiritual deadness is lack of appetite for God. That does not automatically imply a lack of appetite for church. Many people get God and church confused. It is relatively simple to have a regular church appetite, for a number of reasons, without having an appetite for God. Some people have a church appetite because church attendance is a social occasion or because it adds to their prestige. Or maybe because it makes them feel good to go and they like the music. But God does not enter into their reckoning. No hunger for God means no spiritual appetite, and that usually means spiritual deadness.

The Bible is a bore to many people, although Christ said that it is more important than our daily bread. There are thousands of people who have absolutely no hunger or appetite for the Word of God. They have a copy in their homes but they seldom read it. They have no appetite. No appetite can mean no life, and no life always means death. So you see how easy it is to diagnose if you are dead. Check on your appetite for God or your lack of it. Check on your hunger for the Word of God.

When Lazarus was alive he was an active man. The moment he died all trace of activity ceased. This is exactly what happens to a person who is spiritually dead. There is a complete absence of spiritual activity. Physical activity and social activity are common evidences of physical life and social life. But a life that is spent working for success, profit and pleasure, and is never invested in activity on behalf of God's kingdom, is a dead life.

Did you ever hear someone say, "I'm too busy with my profession to get involved in a youth program. I am sorry because I would like to help but you know how it is. Not enough hours in the week!" This is not an unreasonable situation because many people are desperately busy. But the same man will make time for golf and bowling, put in a few hours in front of the television set and never miss a football game. His problem is not too few hours in the week. His problem is that he has no appetite for the sort of activity that is spiritual. We cannot criticize him because of his lack of activity, we can only sympathize, because his lack of activity is a fair indication of his lack of spiritual life. The man is dead.

Martha and Mary loved Lazarus and I am sure that their love was returned. When Lazarus died, however, he no longer seemed to be aware of them. Of course not! There is no awareness in a dead man! Dead men don't love, dead men don't see danger, dead men are unmoved by humor, and pathos doesn't do a thing to them. Dead men are utterly insensitive to what is going on around them. Now this lack of awareness and this absence of sensitivity can be translated into the spiritual realm too. When spiritual realities fail to excite men or to move them it is an ominous sign. Men can measure things from a physical standpoint and evaluate them from the social point of view, but when they are incapable of evaluating and measuring things on a spiritual basis it is serious.

Sometimes parents who have ambitions for their children fight their children if they express a desire to be missionaries. "No child of mine is going to bury himself in that God-forsaken hole," they say, "after all I have spent on his education. Do you really think that I am going to allow this blatant waste of his potential?" These are the words of a person who is no doubt extremely astute, but totally unaware of spiritual realities. This is the language of a dead man!

Lack of appetite, activity and awareness are symptoms of death whether it be in the physical or the spiritual realm. Most people are conscious of a lack in their lives, but they do not know what it is they lack. "Something is missing in my life," they say, or "I am looking for something but I don't know what." Now, of course, if people are made capable of enjoying spiritual life, but have lost this spiritual life, it is not surprising that they say something is missing. Many people who admit that there is something missing also realize that it is missing in the area of their spirit. There are hundreds of people who do not agree. However, it is true to say that there is more or less general agreement on the deadness in the center of many lives even though there is by no means agreement on its cause or its cure.

"People need a good example" cry the well-meaning do-gooders and they do their best to provide this good example. Men and women who give a good example to their fellow citizens are a tremendous boon to society. But did you ever try to give a dead man a good example? Of course we know that this is hopeless.

Someone else will come on the scene and say, "Oh, no, he doesn't need an example, he needs encouragement." You know as well as I do that you can be as enthusiastic and encouraging as it is possible to be, but you will never encourage a dead man to be anything but dead.

On the other hand, social workers with an eye on living conditions and the related behavior of some of the less fortunate say, "Change their environment and all will be well." "Education will do the trick," enthuse others. I expect by the time you have tried examples and enthusiasm and education and environment with no response from a dead man you have grown very discouraged. Many wonderful people have grown utterly disillusioned with the human race. The reason they have been disillusioned is that they have failed to understand that the problem with the human race is a spiritual one.

If a man is dead you cannot expect anything from him. If you don't expect anything from him you will be neither surprised nor disappointed.

All these worthy aids to life will do wonders in certain circumstances, but not one of them or all of them together will do a thing for a dead man. There is only one thing that a dead man needs. *Life!* If men are spiritually dead there is only one thing that they need. Spiritual life.

In this lovely story of the dealing of the Lord Jesus with Lazarus we see a perfect illustration of how spiritual life is made available to a man who is spiritually dead. Jesus Christ Himself claimed to be the life that spiritually dead men needed. He started off by explaining that the reason He came into the world was that He might give men life and "life more abundant." He then further explained, "I am the Resurrection and the Life." Now this Jesus, who is the resurrection and the life, came to the place of Lazarus' burial. He stood outside his tomb and wept. Death in the tomb — and life outside the tomb. What a moment, full of dramatic possibilities! Then Jesus took the initiative and cried with a loud voice "Lazarus come forth." This is exactly what can and ought to happen to dead men today.

The place of your spiritual deadness is your daily existence. Your physical body is the tomb of your spiritual death. Then Jesus who died for you and rose again and who now lives in the power of an endless life is prepared to come right where you are and speak with you. His message is basically simple. "Lazarus. . . .," but perhaps your name is not Lazarus. "Bill, Jack, Marilyn, Jean. . . ." The word of the Lord must come to you personally. He wants you to admit to being dead personally. Then He wants you to be ready to realize your need of Him to be life in the place of your deadness.

The next thing the Lord said was, "Come forth." Now Lazarus had to do something. As the loud clear voice of the Lord penetrated his deadness he had to react against or respond to the authoritative command. This is exactly what you have to do also. If you understand that He has something to say to you and you can understand what He is saying then you must act upon it. Respond to His offer to live within you and commit your life to Him in order that His life in all the power of His resurrection might be released in you through His Holy Spirit. Alternatively, you can reject His call and command to you and remain in your deadness.

Lazarus obeyed the command, responded to the call, and "he that was dead came forth."

Points to Ponder

1. "But she that liveth in pleasure is dead while she liveth" (I Timothy 5:6).
2. "And you hath he quickened, who were dead in trespasses and sins" (Ephesians 2:1).
3. "I am come that they might have life, and that they might have it more abundantly" (John 10:10b).
4. "Jesus said unto her, I am the resurrection, and the life: he that believeth in me, though he were dead, yet shall he live" (John 11:25).
5. Dead men have no *Appetite*
   no *Activity*
   no *Awareness*
6. Dead men need *Life*.

A Prayer to Pray

O God, I think I am spiritually dead for I have no evidence of spiritual life. I understand that Christ came to give life to dead men. Please show me how He can give life to me. In His Name. Amen.

Chapter 2

There was a man of the Pharisees, named Nicodemus, a ruler of the Jews:

The same came to Jesus by night, and said unto him, Rabbi, we know that thou art a teacher come from God: for no man can do these miracles that thou doest, except God be with him.

Jesus answered and said unto him, Verily, verily, I say unto thee, Except a man be born again, he cannot see the kingdom of God.

Nicodemus saith unto him, How can a man be born when he is old? can he enter the second time into his mother's womb, and be born?

Jesus answered, Verily, verily, I say unto thee, Except a man be born of water and of the Spirit, he cannot enter into the kingdom of God.

That which is born of the flesh is flesh, and that which is born of the Spirit is spirit.

Marvel not that I said unto thee, Ye must be born again.

The wind bloweth where it listeth, and thou hearest the sound thereof, but canst not tell whence it cometh, and whither it goeth: so is every one that is born of the Spirit.

Nicodemus answered and said unto him, How can these things be?

Jesus answered and said unto him, Art thou a master of Israel, and knowest not these things?

Verily, verily, I say unto thee, We speak that we do know, and testify that we have seen; and ye receive not our witness.

If I have told you earthly things, and ye believe not, how shall ye believe, if I tell you of heavenly things?

And no man hath ascended up to heaven, but he that came down from heaven, even the Son of man which is in heaven.

And as Moses lifted up the serpent in the wilderness, even so must the Son of man be lifted up:

That whosoever believeth in him should not perish, but have eternal life.

For God so loved the world, that he gave his only begotten Son, that whosoever believeth in him should not perish, but have everlasting life.

John 3:1-16

2

The Quandary of a Dead Man

NICODEMUS WAS DEAD AND DIDN'T KNOW IT. BUT HE SHOULD HAVE known. He had a brilliant intellect, in fact he was professor of theology at the University of Jerusalem. His training had been of the highest caliber and he was an outstanding man. It is tragic to know that outstanding men are sometimes dead men, but it is worse to think that they can know so much and yet be so ignorant. Some brilliant men don't even know the truth about themselves! Imagine Nicodemus all those years addressing his students and being dead all that time! He may not have known but I wonder if his students knew?

For the whole of his life he had meticulously observed all the rules of his religion. And those rules were tough. Carefully he checked on the food he ate, the company he kept, the places he went and the clothes he wore. His religion ruled all these things and many more. He must have been so sincere and so serious, and yet so very dead. When he spoke in the Sanhedrin, the place of government for his country, he spoke with a great concern for truth and honesty. His integrity was unquestioned, and he was held in high esteem. But the tragedy of the man was that he wanted to help govern his country when he couldn't govern himself. And this was because he didn't know the most important thing about himself. He was dead!

One dark night he learned the truth. As an honest, intelligent man he had been most interested in the activities of a young carpenter-preacher who had been making a name for Himself. He decided to have a personal talk with the young Man. Of course, a man in his position had to be careful. What would the officials of the university think if they knew that he was consorting with an uneducated artisan! It wouldn't be so good if the Sanhedrin found out that he had met with a potential rabble rouser either. Of course the Pharisees didn't miss too many tricks, and Nicodemus knew that he would be the talk of the synagogue if they found out where he had been. So once again, proving that discretion is the better part of valor, he slipped furtively into the presence of the young Galilean, under cover of darkness.

Nicodemus was most gracious. He, the professor, addressed the young carpenter-preacher as "Rabbi." Then he complimented Him on His miracles, and acknowledged that this man, years his junior, was undoubtedly God's Man of the moment. He was shaken to the depths by the response to his compliments. "Unless you are born again, you will never see the kingdom of God." I have often wondered why the Lord Jesus was so blunt on this occasion. Was He conscious that Nicodemus wanted to talk theology and He wanted to deal with the man's soul? I don't know, but I do know that He had no intention of wasting time on trivialities. Here was a key man of learning, position and integrity who was as dead as it was possible to be, and something needed to be done — and quick!

Now Nicodemus knew many things about God. No doubt he had lectured on His names and titles many times. He knew the divine attributes and promises, and was fully conversant with the theological concept of the kingdom of God. Now the young preacher told the old professor he might have lectured on it, but he couldn't possibly understand it if he had never been born again. This was shattering news.

Nicodemus thought that he had been in the kingdom since he was eight days old. All his school days he had been thinking in terms of training in order to serve the Kingdom. He had done well in his service from a human point of view. He was a success, and he was firmly sitting on the top of the tree! But if the carpenter was right, he hadn't even seen the Kingdom. All these years he had been on the wrong tack!

Dead he was, but he certainly wasn't stupid. At first glance his response to the "born again" statement looked stupid. "How can a man, when he is old, enter his mother's womb and be born?" No, Nicodemus wasn't asking a stupid question. I think he was being sarcastic. He was probably thinking something like this — "Young Man, are you trying to be funny? I came here for an intelligent conversation and You start talking nonsense. Born again indeed! What do You think I am? Do You want me back in embryo form?"

Totally unmoved, the Lord said, "Unless you are born of water and the Spirit, you cannot enter the kingdom." In effect

He was saying, "Nicodemus, I want you to understand that there is something worse than being unable to *see* the kingdom of God, and that is being unable to *enter* it." Of course, some of the confusion in the mind of Nicodemus was undoubtedly caused by the fact that his idea of the kingdom of God and Christ's conception of the Kingdom were totally different. Therefore, while they were both using the same term, they were thinking of different things. Nicodemus the politician may have been thinking primarily in terms of a political kingdom with a king sitting on a throne in Jerusalem. Were Roman conquerors of his beloved country in his thoughts? Was he interested in ousting them from the land? David the great king and his successors and the possibilities of the kingdom being restored perhaps were what he had in mind.

Little wonder then that he was having difficulty understanding why it was necessary to be "born again" to get into *that* kingdom! The theologian in him had some idea of the kingdom of God being more than just political. He believed that when God's king reigned politically from Jerusalem then God would be reigning in the world. As far as he was concerned, the king of the Jews was God's agent and when the earthly king was on the throne in the holy city then God was reigning through him. Then all the subjects of the earthly king would, through him, be subject to God and, accordingly, in the kingdom.

When two men have a conversation, and one of them does not understand the terms that the other is using, it is more than difficult to get very far. Nicodemus understood neither the term, "the kingdom of God," nor what it meant to be "born again." So you see it wasn't surprising that he was in a quandary about "Except a man be born again, he cannot see the kingdom of God."

The Lord took the initiative and began to explain further. He used the simple analogy of human birth to explain what He meant by the new birth. "That which is born of the flesh is flesh; and that which is born of the Spirit is spirit," He said.

"When a baby is born it receives life." But the Lord wasn't talking about physical life any more than He was talking about a political kingdom. He was talking about spiritual life — the life from God deep in the recesses of a man's spirit that makes God real and allows God to be king in the center of a man's life. When a baby is born, it is suddenly conscious of a new world.

At first it looks decidedly uninterested in life and almost appears to regret having arrived. But baby can see and hear and very soon baby begins to know and to understand. That which is born physically is purely physical, but that which is born of the Spirit is spiritual. There is such a thing as spiritual seeing and hearing. A born-again soul can see and understand, often in a remarkable way, deep things of God. They become real to him. Truths that were once dark now become crystal clear. A dull Bible becomes a blazing Book.

When baby arrives he is the latest member of the family. Sometimes we get the impression that baby is the most important member of the family. But whatever the status of the new arrival, there is no doubt that family membership is automatically involved in getting born. God becomes man's Father in a wonderfully close relationship when man is born again by the Spirit into the family of God. All the joys and privileges of family relationship in the greatest and most wonderful family belong to those born into God's family. The family has its origins in God. It reaches all classes through all ages in all lands and will last for all time and then be endless in eternity. The family of God is fabulous, and God is its Father. His concern is the raising of His children. He cares and protects. His guidance is assured and He provides all that His children need. In the same way that earthly children love and respect their fathers, the children of God reverence and adore the Lord who made them His children. His home is their home. His wealth is theirs. All that He has is available to them as they learn to enjoy it and all that they are comes under His benevolent control. Their good is His concern and His delight is their concern. Brothers and sisters abound. Wherever a member of the family goes in all corners of the world the family will be represented. Strangers to each other will be knit together in moments when a common bond is discovered through a common relationship to a common Father. The birth of a dead man spiritually is dramatic, climactic, thrilling and reaches further than any man can envisage age.

In essence the message of the Lord was, "Don't be surprised, Nicodemus, I'm not talking about a physical kingdom. I'm dealing with something spiritual. Nicodemus, when I say that you must be born again, I mean exactly what I say. You *must* be born again. It is absolutely imperative. If you ever want to understand the mysteries of God, and experience the reality of

God, you must be born again. If you want to enter the kingdom and join the family you must be born again. Because, Nicodemus, there is no other entrance to the realm of God's reign
and the membership of God's family. The new birth is the only
gateway."

Scratching his head, with his brow plowed with puzzled
furrows, Nicodemus asked "How?" "How can these things be?"
This is always the quandary of a dead man. "How can I be
born again? How can a man who is physically alive and spiritually dead receive new life? How?" "Do you mean to tell Me
that you, the teacher of Israel, do not know how to be born
again?" said the Lord. Evidently the nation was at a low spiritual
ebb if the top teacher didn't know how to be born again!
When the leaders of the church don't know the basics of spiritual
experience it is a sad and dangerous day for the nation. Any
nation is blind if it is led by the blind. Dead men don't lead
dead men very effectively. Jesus lived in such a day, and in
some ways so do we.

The Lord then reproached Nicodemus for failing to accept
the clear teaching of the prophets and disciples not to mention
His own teaching. "What is the point of Me telling you heavenly things, Nicodemus, if you refuse to accept the things you
have been taught so far?" Notice that there was a degree of rejection and a certain amount of pride in this sincere man.
For some reason he had not been prepared to go along with
the teachings to which he had been exposed. In all probability
the reasons stemmed from pride. They usually do. The reasons
for refusing the truth come in various forms but have the
same core. Pride doesn't like to be told it is dead. Pride thinks
it is sufficient and adequate. But deadness means a lack of life,
and this is the worst kind of insufficiency. Pride thinks, "I am
good enough for the Kingdom, in fact, the Kingdom ought to be
thankful it is honored by my presence." So pride doesn't like to
be told, "You won't even be in the Kingdom." Pride says, "I'm
not perfect," but always gets upset when someone says, "That's
right, you are not!" There was a certain pride in Nicodemus
that was quite understandable, but that doesn't mean it was
excusable.

So Nicodemus needed to be told that spiritual experience
comes through "water and the Spirit." There has been much
discussion about the interpretation of the word "water" in this
context. It would seem to me that the meaning the Lord had in

mind was something that Nicodemus would understand by the term "water." I think that there is little doubt that Nicodemus, being a religious, educated Jew, would realize that it meant some kind of washing and purifying. To his mind, I feel the statement meant, "You must be washed and made clean before you can come into the Kingdom — clean from pride and arrogance. You must be purified from the idea that you are good enough even though God says that you are not."

Evidently Nicodemus accepted this, for the Lord proceeded. (There is no point in proceeding with an explanation of the new birth if people refuse to accept the fact of their sin and the necessity for repentance and cleansing.) He proceeded by means of an illustration very familiar to the professor. Out of the professor's textbook He took the story of the children of Israel in the wilderness. They had rebelled, and they had rejected the instructions of God and were living in a disgruntled and perplexed state. Barren and unyielding, the wilderness stretched on all sides and they were ripe for rebellion. The serpents came in among them and hundreds were bitten. The poison flowed in their bodies and death was inevitable. They were as good as dead when Moses once again acted on the people's behalf and spoke to the Lord. Moses was told to make a serpent of brass and lift it high on a pole. Then with a loud, clear voice he told the people that God promised new life to all who would look to the serpent, the symbol of God's promise, and trust God to do what He promised. There was nothing new to Nicodemus in this story, but the application was new!

"In the same way that Moses lifted up the serpent, Nicodemus, I am going to be lifted up," said the Lord. This was a clear allusion to the impending crucifixion of the Lord Jesus. Evidently Nicodemus had either already heard an explanation of this, or he was given an explanation at this juncture which was not recorded by John. In any case Nicodemus must have heard about the uplifting of the Son of man that was to have such far-reaching effects.

The Lord was saying that His death on a cross was going to be the means of forgiveness for all those bitten by the disease of sin and suffering — the deadness of spirit that sin brings. His death was to take place in order that sin might be judged and sinners forgiven by God.

Of course Nicodemus knew that some people refused to look at the serpent, and as a result they died. Others said that they couldn't understand how a piece of twisted metal on a stick could get poison out of their veins. They died. Some felt that if they couldn't be healed by their own doctors they certainly weren't going to expose themselves to a quack physician holding a pole in the air. They died. Nicodemus also knew that there was a real danger that he might adopt a similar attitude to the remarkable story of this remarkable young Man. This young Man hadn't died, and yet He wanted him to believe that His death would do something for him that his religion had failed to do. He knew, that, while he had very real reservations, he certainly had no answer to the young Man's authority nor had he any alternative to what the young Man was offering. Nicodemus decided to be careful that he did not reject the message because he couldn't understand it or because he did not like it! It was important that he did not forget the men in the desert who did that and perished!

Deep in his heart Nicodemus knew that the deadness of his spirit was simply the introduction to what the Lord called "perishing." But the Lord said that instead of perishing he could have eternal life. Perhaps Nicodemus was confused on the subject of eternal life. In fact I am sure that he was! Confusion or not, the offer was stupendous. He was being told in all seriousness and sincerity that if he would only trust himself to the Christ who was to die for him, then his sins would be cleansed. Not only that, but he would pick himself up off the sandy barren floor of his desert and step out in newness of life. A new life – the commencement of which could only be described as being born again. The born again part of it was to come through the imparting of the life of God – eternal life. This life would be born in him through the Spirit of God. And it was all for him if he would only take his eyes off himself and look to the One who was going to die for him.

The pressure of those moments must have been intense. Imagine the eminent man confronted with the fact of his own deadness – haunted by his ineffectiveness – baffled by the news of his error and now firmly confronted with the necessity of deciding what he was going to do. The quiet compelling gaze of the Lord and the stillness of the night contrasted dramatically with the turmoil of his own heart and the sting of his conscience.

It is no light thing to be told you are dead. It is no easy matter to decide what you are going to do with the offer of a new start and a new life through a new birth. To receive the life of the risen Christ, and to enjoy the forgiveness of sins that He offers is a tremendous step. Strong men have sweated and brave men have trembled when told that if they want new life they need new birth, and new birth means a new start in a new kingdom with a new King. They know who their king is, and they are familiar with his demands. They know the changes that must be made if he is to be dethroned and God is to be enthroned. Nicodemus was on the spot. What should he do? This is the quandary of a dead man.

Points to Ponder

1. "Jesus answered and said, Verily, verily, I say unto thee, Except a man be born again, he cannot see the kingdom of God" (John 3:3).
2. "Jesus answered, Verily, verily, I say unto thee, Except a man be born of water and of the Spirit, he cannot enter into the kingdom of God" (John 3:5).
3. "Marvel not that I said unto thee, Ye must be born again" (John 3:7).
4. "How can these things be?" (John 3:9).
5. "For God so loved the world, that he gave his only begotten Son, that whosoever believeth in him should not perish, but have everlasting life" (John 3:16).
6. "It is no easy matter to decide what you are going to do with the offer of a new start and a new life through a new birth."

A Prayer to Pray

Dear Lord, I know I am dead and I know that I need life. I realize that Christ died and rose again to give me life. Help me to be willing to be made anew for His sake. Amen.

Chapter 3

And when he was gone forth into the way, there came one running, and kneeled to him, and asked him, Good Master, what shall I do that I may inherit eternal life?

And Jesus said unto him, Why callest thou me good? there is none good but one, that is, God.

Thou knowest the commandments, Do not commit adultery, Do not kill, Do not steal, Do not bear false witness, Defraud not, Honour thy father and mother.

And he answered and said unto him, Master, all these have I observed from my youth.

Then Jesus beholding him loved him, and said unto him, One thing thou lackest: go thy way, sell whatsoever thou hast, and give to the poor, and thou shalt have treasure in heaven: and come, take up the cross, and follow me.

And he was sad at that saying, and went away grieved: for he had great possesssions.

Mark 10:17-22

3

The Choice of a Dead Man

THE SANHEDRIN HAD NO SHORTAGE OF PUZZLED MEMBERS WHEN Jesus was going about His business. Nicodemus wasn't the only one to come to Him to discuss his problems. Another eminent ruler came to the Lord one day, but under totally different circumstances. He came in full daylight, right out in the open, unlike Nicodemus who crept in by night! More than that, he actually came running! Surely a most undignified method of transport for a member of the Sanhedrin! But he didn't just run!

When he arrived at the place where the Lord was sitting, to everyone's astonishment, he threw himself at the Master's feet and knelt before Him. This young gentleman was in dead earnest. He didn't care who saw him. It didn't matter to him what people thought of his behavior. His status was forgotten. He was oblivious to the dust on his clothes and to the stares of the passersby. There was something so important on his mind that he counted everything else to be irrelevant. How exciting to hear of someone who thought the Lord was so important that he forgot everything and went to Him!

What was on his mind? The first words from his lips give the answer. Eternal life! "Good Master, what must I do that I may inherit eternal life?" he asked as he stopped in front of Christ.

This is a most remarkable question and one of utmost importance. There are many people who do not know what eternal life is and because they aren't sure what it is they don't know if they have it. Obviously, if they don't know this they cannot possibly know if they want it! Others have some ideas about it, but they don't know how to get it. Still more people think that it is something they may get when they die — if they have been good enough.

Our young friend, however, knew quite a few things about

eternal life. He knew it existed. He knew he didn't have it. He knew he wanted it. And he knew where to find it. So he knew a lot!

Presumably he had heard the Lord speaking on the subject at some time. From what he had heard it was clear to him that there was much more to life than he was experiencing. Isn't it sad that this is true of many wonderful people alive at the present time? They are wonderful — but dead.

The Bible says, "These things I have written . . . that you might know that you have eternal life" (I John 5:13). Notice that it does not say ". . . hope that you might get." "Know" instead of "hope." "Have" instead of "may get." Do you know that you have eternal life? If you are not sure then your place is beside the young ruler at the Master's feet, inquiring.

Eternal life is not a thing. It is not strictly an "it." Eternal life is a Person. Talking about the Lord Jesus the Bible says, "This is the true God, and eternal life" (I John 5:20). It is not difficult to see that the term eternal life is basically the same as "life of the eternal One." To have eternal life is to have the life of the eternal One. Not to have eternal life is obviously to be without the eternal One and His life. And to be without His life is to be dead.

If it is possible for a human being to experience the life of the eternal One within him in exchange for his spiritual deadness, it is obvious that eternal life is not only important because it lasts a long time. It lasts an eternity which is endless. Nothing lasts longer than that! There is quantity in greatest measure, but it is the quality that is so wonderful. Eternal life is life that lasts for eternity and springs from the Person of God Himself. It is the life of God through the Lord Jesus imparted to people while they are still here on earth. Eternal life has all the quality of His life.

This young man had seen the quality of the life that the Master lived and he knew that his life didn't bear comparison. Yet he had everything, and the Master had very little. Jesus wandered about homeless, but he had a fine home. The Lord had to be continually on His guard because of people who wanted to kill Him, but the young man was living in the lap of luxury. In fact, the strange sense of dissatisfaction that he was experiencing was even the more remarkable because he had everything that anyone could ever desire. His neighbors envied him! "If I had his position I would be happy." "Boy, is he rich!"

"If only I had his money and his looks and his personality and his prestige, I would be the happiest man on earth." Youth and money and home and position were all on his side. Security and popularity were his. But his life lacked quality. There was no real sense of belonging. He was empty.

When he came in search of eternal life, he was searching for a life that he had heard the Master had come to give — "life more abundant." That was what he didn't have and that was what he wanted. The eternal life he sought was a life of eternal quality. He wanted to live and he knew that the life he wanted was to be found only in the Eternal One. Do you have that kind of life? Do you have a life that is as eternal in its quality as it is in its quantity? If not, then your place is beside the young man at the Master's feet. Your question ought to be, "What must I do to inherit eternal life?"

Jesus started to answer in an indirect sort of way. "Why do you call me good?" Then He said, "There is none good but God." Why would he say that? Surely the young man was only being polite!

Evidently the Lord realized that the young man needed to learn that although he was good, he was not good enough! When Jesus talked to Nicodemus He bluntly introduced the subject of the new birth. On this occasion He did a similar thing. There is much to be said for getting to the point as quickly as possible! Among other things it saves time! Not good enough? But this young man was outstanding. Listen to the conversation.

"You know the commandments don't you?"

"Yes, Master."

"Don't commit adultery."

"I haven't."

"Don't kill."

"I haven't."

Through the list went the Lord, looking the young man straight in the eye. Under this gaze, a gaze that can strip a man naked to his inner thoughts, the young man never flinched once. "I have kept them all since I was a youth," he said. The Lord was impressed with this fine young man. He felt a tremendous surge of love in His heart for him. But still he wasn't good enough. The lesson the Lord had to teach him was that it is possible to be good, but not good enough. The world is full of "good people" but they aren't good enough.

How can this be? It all depends on the standard of meas-

urement. You might be a good swimmer in the pool next door.
When people see you cut through the water for about six strokes
they say, "What a good swimmer." But how would you make out
in the Olympics? Would you be good in the pool next door
but way out of your class at the Olympics? You would be good,
but not good enough! The young man was outstanding by
human standards. His friends called him religious. His em-
ployees called him "fair and kind." His business associates
commented on his honesty. But God saw his weakness.

Do you know what his weakness was? The Lord didn't tell
him in words. He proved it to him another way. "There's only
one thing lacking, young man. I'll tell you what to do if you
want to have this life of eternal quality and quantity. Go home
and put your home up for sale. When it is sold, give the money
away, and then come back to me and we can talk business."

The ruler's weakness lay in his possessions. "Money is the
root of all evil," is one of the most misleading misquotes of
Scripture. The Bible does not say that. It says, "The love of
money is the root of all evil" (I Timothy 6:10). There is nothing
sinful about money, and there is nothing sinful in having money.
But there lies untold danger in loving it and living for it. Men
will lie for it, cheat for it, scheme for it, even kill for it. When
a man begins to love his money and his possessions more than
anything else he makes a god out of them. That is where the
sin lies.

The young man looked as if the bottom had fallen out of
his world. "Sell my possessions and give everything away? But
that's unthinkable, it's unreasonable, I couldn't possibly do that!"

The Lord had examined him on the commandments and
he had come through with flying colors. However, He had not
mentioned the great commandment that stated, "Thou shalt have
no other gods before me." If He had talked about this the
young man would have said, "I've never done that. I have never
bowed the knee to Baal. I have never worshiped the gods of
gold and silver." But this would have been untrue. He had never
been anything but orthodox in his religion, but at the same time
his orthodoxy had left plenty of room for other gods. He had
worshiped the gods of gold and silver. He didn't realize this
until he was told to get rid of them. He only learned how
precious they were when he was threatened with the possibility
of having to do without them. His love and devotion only became apparent when he saw that he couldn't live without them.

His worship and dependence had never been so real until the ghastly moment when he was confronted with his own slavery to these things. The one God was his god, but only in theory. His money was his god in practice.

It is so simple to be good by the low standards of modern society, and it is impossible to be good by God's standards. This does not mean that God is unreasonable. On the contrary, God loved this young man and longed to do something for him. But you can't do anything for a person who is not prepared to admit that there is something wrong with him! The thing that was wrong with this earnest, good young man was that he was governed by sin. The greatest sin that man can perpetrate is to deny God the right to be God in his life. This was his sin, and this is the sin of most of the people you ever meet. Eternal life is available to sinners, but first the sinners must admit that they are sinners. Then they must be prepared to turn from their sin. It is so clear in the case of the rich young ruler. First he had to recognize that he was giving nothing more than lip service to his God. Then he had to admit it was sin, and to be ready, whatever the consequences, to turn from his sinful approach to life. Only when this was done was the Lord prepared to do business with him. With these tremendous truths ringing in his ears the young man was hardly ready to take any more. But the Master hadn't finished with him by any means.

He went on to explain that a person who desires eternal life must also, "take up the cross and follow me" (Mark 10:21). Many remarkable things have been said about this phrase "taking up the cross." I have heard some people who are afflicted with arthritis saying, "I suppose there is nothing much that I can do about it. It must be my cross so I'll just have to grin and bear it." I don't want to appear unsympathetic to any sufferers, but I must say that their arthritis is not their cross. It is simply their arthritis. You see the big thing to remember is this. Often when we talk about bearing the cross we think that it means putting up with the unavoidable things of life with the bravest smile possible. No, this is not cross-bearing. When the Lord Jesus took up His cross He wasn't putting up with something that He couldn't escape. He wasn't trying to look as if He were enjoying it when He wasn't. He was abandoning Himself to His Father's will, and that will included a cross. He took it as a token of His overall acceptance of God's will for His life even though it was going to be severely painful. To take up the cross means that you do what Jesus did. You recognize the Lordship of the Lord, surrender to His will, and do it regardless of the consequences.

Occasionally you may hear people talking about the cost of becoming a Christian. Then in the next breath they will tell you that salvation is free! "Eternal life is a gift but there is a price to pay," they exclaim. Now how it can be a gift and also require payment I haven't yet been able to discover. We know what they mean. They are pointing out, quite rightly, that accepting the gift of eternal life affects a person in all that he says and does. Some requirements are hard, and therefore are regarded as part of the price that has to be paid. I think a better way of looking at it would be to realize that all the price has been paid – by Christ. Having paid the price of our ransom from sin by death Christ rose again to offer us life through a relationship with Him. Eternal life is based absolutely on Him. If there is no relationship, there is no eternal life. Obviously if eternal life is based on a relationship to Him, He is perfectly entitled to state the terms of the relationship. His terms are quite straightforward. He expects us to be related to Him as He is, not how we want Him to be. He is Lord, and therefore eternal life is a relationship to the Lord which automatically involves acknowledging His Lordship. That isn't the cost! It is purely an elementary aspect of the relationship!

But that is not all! The Lord is not remotely interested in a snap decision that doesn't develop into an attitude of life. "And follow me," He added. This means that He instructed the young candidate for eternal life to be prepared for a totally new life – prepared to go where his Lord led him. It was going to involve a "going on." New avenues and possibilities were to be explored. Fresh areas of life and adventure were to be opened up as the Lord directed. He had to be ready for anything that the Lord might have in mind.

This was hard for the young man. He rose to his feet. His lined face betrayed the battle raging in his heart. He was torn. He knew what he wanted. He knew he could get it. He knew how it worked. He knew what to do. He knew all that he needed to know. But knowing wasn't enough. Now he had to do what he knew. The decision was all his and only his. Not a soul could help him. Not even the Lord could do a thing for him. The Lord was able to do all things, and still is, but He will not break His own rules. And one of His rules is that He allows man the right to choose. Therefore, the young man had the right to choose and the responsibility to choose right. Slowly he turned away, and he spoke not a word. His shoulders hunched, his feet dragged in the dust. He decided in that moment to say "No" to life. Automatically he said "Yes" to death. He walked away from eternal life. He walked away dead!

Points to Ponder

1. "Good Master, what shall I do that I may inherit eternal life" (I John 5:20b).
2. "For the wages of sin is death; but the gift of God is eternal life through Jesus Christ our Lord" (Romans 6:23).
3. ". . . his Son Jesus Christ. This is the true God, and eternal life" (I John 5:20b).
4. "And this is the record, that God hath given to us eternal life, and this life is in his Son. He that hath the Son hath life; and he that hath not the Son of God hath not life. These things have I written unto you that believe on the name of the Son of God; that ye may know that ye have eternal life, and that ye may believe on the name of the Son of God" (I John 5:11-13).
5. To take up the cross means that you do what Jesus did. Recognize the Lordship of the Lord, surrender to His will and do it regardless of the consequences.
6. "And follow me, He added. This means that he instructed the young candidate for eternal life to be prepared for a totally new life – prepared to go where this Lord led him. It was going to involve "a going on."

A Prayer to Pray

Dear Lord, Thank You that You offer eternal life to me as a gift. I know that it involves a relationship with Yourself. Teach me all that it means to be ready to take up the cross and follow in order that I might enjoy Your life in me which is life eternal through Jesus Christ our Lord. Amen.

Chapter 4

I appeal to you for my [own spiritual] child, Onesimus [meaning profitable], whom I have begotten [in the faith] while a captive in these chains.

Once he was unprofitable to you, but now he is indeed profitable to you as well as to me.

I am sending him back to you in his own person (and it is like sending) my very heart.

I would have chosen to keep him with me, in order that he might minister to my needs in your stead during my imprisonment for the Gospel's sake.

But it has been my wish to do nothing about it without first consulting you *and* getting your consent, in order that your benevolence might not seem to be the result of compulsion *or* of pressure but might be voluntary [on your part].

Perhaps it was for this reason that he was separated [from you] for a while, that you might have him back as yours forever.

Not as a slave any longer but as [something] more than a slave, as a brother [Christian], especially dear to me but how much more to you, both in the flesh [as a servant] and in the Lord [as a fellow believer].

If then you consider me a partner *and* a comrade in fellowship, welcome *and* receive him as you would [welcome and receive] me.

And if he has done you any wrong in any way, or owes anything [to you], charge that to my account.

I, Paul, write it with my own hand, I promise to repay it [in full] — and that is to say nothing [of the fact] that you owe me your very self!

Yes, brother, let me have some profit from you in the Lord. Cheer *and* refresh my heart in Christ.

Philemon 10-20 (Amplified Bible)

4

The Steps of a Dead Man

ONESIMUS WAS HIS NAME. A MOST UNUSUAL NAME BY PRESENT day tastes, and I should imagine it was rather unique in his day, too! It means "profitable." Imagine the fun his friends may have had teasing him about his name! Think of the agony he might have suffered as a boy. Every time he did something wrong at school he braced himself for the inevitable jibes about "profitability" that came his way.

As time went on it became obvious that young "profitable" wasn't living up to his name. He became a slave in the household of a religious gentleman called Philemon. It was soon apparent that he wasn't going to get along there too well. It could have been the religious atmosphere of the household that got on his nerves. There is nothing quite so irritating as being exposed to religious people in a religious environment, and being thoroughly irreligious yourself. Many people have found this experience extremely trying. Such was the unhappy lot of young Onesimus.

Naturally he had many things for which to be eternally grateful. For instance, he had a master who was an outstanding Christian gentleman. His conditions of service were as ideal as it was possible for them to be in those days of slavery. He could have been in far less pleasant circumstances, and even if he didn't appreciate the Christianity he certainly benefited from the Christian graces of his master.

Onesimus' main problem was that he had much religion, but no reality. He was the dead man we have been considering. He had no shortage of encouragement, as well as Christian education and an ideal environment coupled with an outstanding example, but he lacked life. Poor old "profitable" was dead. Because the religion that he saw lacked reality for him, he had to do something about it. Being a lively young man he did the predictable thing. He rebelled. Often I have seen young people exposed to and sometimes hammered by religion that was meaningless to them. Nine times out of ten they have rebelled. In fact, I believe that if a young person has any "spirit" in him at all, he will most likely rebel against religion that appears to him to be suited to the elderly middle classes rather than the up and coming young people who have their lives to live.

Living his life was uppermost in Onesimus' mind as one would expect. He didn't relish the thought of surrendering to the God of whom he had heard so much. He found that there were many more attractive ways of living his life open to him. Religion on the outside, and latent rebellion on the inside, meant a most uncomfortable turmoil for the young slave. I expect he made many other people uncomfortable at the same time!

It only needed a spark to cause the explosion. The Bible story spares us the details, but not the results. Onesimus decided that enough was enough, and he exploded. He decided to pack his bags and leave Philemon and Colosse and religion and get out into the big world and live. The craving of the dead is always for life. So he ran to look for it. Notice carefully the progressive experience of this man. Religion without reality led to rebellion that made him run.

Onesimus wasn't just running away from people and situations. He was running away from God. That, of course, is a common phenomenon of the human race, and a ridiculous one as well. It is possible to run away from God, but it is impossible to get away from Him as Onesimus was to discover later. But still the rebellious run. They cannot see that their only hope is in running *to* God rather than running *from* Him. "Come unto me and I will give you. . . ." He says. But in their minds they say, "Let's get as far as possible from Him, because He will rob us of all that we think is important and spoil all that we want to do."

Talking of robbing, of course, leads us to the next part of Onesimus' decline. He was short of funds, and his projected journey required funds. Religion had taught him to respect other people's property, but the pressure was on him. His desire to run was too great. The visions of "life" that he had conjured up in his mind burned brightly. He lost control and he robbed his master. This was also quite predictable. When a man is desperate nothing is sacred. A man's principles are always subject to revision and rejection when there is the possibility of the principle thwarting his desire. He knew better, but he robbed.

In his position as a slave this was about the worst thing he could do. He was doomed. So he ran all the harder.

In a strange sort of way men rob God. In fact, any man who rebels and runs automatically robs God. This may sound ludicrous, but it is perfectly true. Some would even say, "How can a man rob God?" This is exactly what they were saying in Malachi's day. God explained then and His explanation still stands. Man robs God when he keeps to himself what is really God's property. God reminded them about tithing. In those days man was expected to recognize that one tenth of his earnings (before tax!) was not his at all. It was God's. People then were like we are now. They were greedy. So they began to withhold the tenth thinking that they were simply choosing not to give something that belonged to them. But they weren't. They were holding back from God what was His. That is blatant robbery!

God also accused the people of robbing Him in another way. They were giving to Him things that were inferior, such as lame sheep. With a pious smile on their faces, but with a keen eye to business, they offered animals for sacrifice that were of no market value. God called this robbery. This kind of robbery is not uncommon today. Where is the man or woman who can say "I have always given God His due, and have never kept back anything that belongs to Him"? Where are the men and women who can honestly say "I have never relegated God to an inferior place in my life, and I have never given to Him anything but the best"?

"Rome, here I come," was his magnificent obsession. And to Rome he went. He had a great time there, and no doubt thoroughly enjoyed himself. Sometimes you hear preachers saying that people like Onesimus aren't having a good time. These preachers either haven't tried it, or it is so long since they did that they have forgotten what a great time some people do have in their sin. What they probably mean is that the great time doesn't either last or satisfy. Neither does it achieve anything except a transient enjoyment that disappears all too quickly.

Onesimus was having fun, but in the depths of his conscience there was a nagging fear of the consequences of his sin. His enjoyment was constantly flavored with unpleasant thoughts that his inner man wouldn't let him forget. The dead man is happy, when he is happy. It is the times when he doesn't

have the necessary entertainments or distractions that cause him
most trouble. Then his conscience troubles him, and he has no
peace. The conscience of our young friend was spoiling his
vacation in Rome, and there wasn't anything he could do about
it. Then came a remarkable coincidence that wasn't a coincidence!

There is no doubt in my mind that this "coincidence" was
a piece of magnificent engineering. It was the work of a Genius
who was busy bringing two people together, even though neither
knew that the other was in the vicinity. This is part of God's
speciality. He knows the hearts of men, and often better than
the men themselves. He was fully conversant with the inner
workings of young Onesimus, and Onesimus was an open book to
God. The mad search for life that the runaway slave was making
had not escaped the all-seeing eye of the young man's Creator.
Nor had the heart hunger that was driving him remorselessly
into one foolish escapade after another.

God cared in a practical way. So He looked around for
someone whom He could trust to get in touch with the desperate
youth. His choice was Paul. This was apparently a strange
choice. If you were sending someone after a runaway thief,
would you send a theologian? If you needed to cut short the
drunken vacation of a reprobate young man, would you send a
missionary? Perhaps you wouldn't, but God did. It all depends
what you want to do with the youth when you have found
him. If you want to bring him to justice, send a policeman
and try him, and throw him in jail. In Onesimus' case it would
perhaps have meant execution. Or if you want to teach him a
lesson and get him off the drink or drugs, and away from his
unsavory friends, send someone tough who can handle a rough
situation. But God doesn't work our way, because He is interested in achieving more than justice and rehabilitation. He
is concerned about the remaking of ruined lives, not just salvag-
ing them. That being the case, He has to send more than an
officer of the law, or a social worker. A spiritual man is needed
who not only can deal with the legal and social problems of the
case, but also can handle the deep spiritual root cause of the
problems. Paul was the man for the job.

God is expert at organizing the circumstances of men in such
a way that He can do something for them. I remember a few
years ago speaking in a coffee bar full of young people who
would not go near a church. The bar was crowded with all types

of teenagers. I was speaking about Onesimus, and when I had stopped talking, a girl of about 16 years of age came to me and said, "I'm rebelling against everything. I robbed my mother this evening. I took all her money out of her purse. Now I'm on the run." Her story fitted the story I was telling perfectly. She drifted into the coffee bar not knowing anything about it. I spoke about the young man whose experience fitted hers without knowing anything about her. Coincidence? I don't believe so, because God sends men to get in touch with the spiritually desperate.

Now I don't think we have any reason to assume that God said, "Paul, go to Rome, and on the Appian Way you'll find the young slave that you met at the home of Philemon in Colosse. Get him and take him back to Philemon. He's on the run." No, I feel certain that Paul was in Rome as part of God's plan for his life, and that, as always, he had his eyes wide open to opportunities of being an instrument of God's blessing wherever he went. He was so well-acquainted with the strange coincidences that happened in his life with consistent regularity that he now recognized them as part of the divine plan. In fact, he anticipated this sort of thing. He wasn't surprised any more. Paul had long since learned that anything can, and probably will happen when God is in control.

When Paul saw young Onesimus so far from home, and obviously "living it up," his eyes lit up, and he thought, "Hello, and what exactly is that young man doing here?" He found out the easy way by going up to him, and asking him! The youth on the run must have had the biggest shock of his young life. The thing that he had dreaded more than anything else since he went on the run had happened. He had been caught. Immediately he began to wonder how much Paul knew. Had Philemon sent him? Was it any good trying to bluff his way out? "What are you doing here Onesimus?" asked the preacher. "Vacation," might have been the unconvincing answer. I don't know how long it took to get the real story, but eventually it came out. "Paul, I got tired of everything. I wanted to live. I felt as if I was in a straightjacket. I rebelled, and I ran, and I robbed."

Of one thing I am certain. Paul did not say, "Tut, tut," and launch into a three-point sermon! This young man had no need of a sermon. He was caught, and he knew it. He was fully aware of his sin. The awful truth of what he was, and

what he had done filled his mind. "What can I do, Paul?" That
is the question that Paul was waiting for! It is the question
that the Lord loves to hear, for it is the question of a dead
man who is at the point of realization.

All was not as well as he thought. He was in need, and
he didn't know from where his help would come. Simply and
seachingly Paul reminded Onesimus of the things that he had
already heard. "You will have to repent, Onesimus. In case you
aren't sure what it means, it means make an about turn in the
way you are going, and let God be God." Onesimus replied,
"I'll do that." But there was something else that had to be done.
Repentance in his case involved retribution. He had to return
to the place of his crime, and put right what he had done wrong.
He had to repay what he had stolen. Retribution is the "stuff"
of which repentance is made. If you meet someone who claims
to have repented, but who is not prepared to put right what he
has done wrong, then it is doubtful if you have met a real
penitent. "I'm ready for that, Paul. Yes, I'll go to Philemon and
I'll take what's coming to me. But, Paul, I don't know where
I'll find the strength." This was the heartcry of the crestfallen
youth.

He didn't have the strength yet, because he hadn't received
the Lord Jesus through His Spirit to infuse life into his deadness.
He was a stranger to all the strength that the Lord is in the
hearts of all who receive Him. Paul showed him how to thank
Christ for dying for him personally. Then he led him in a simple prayer asking the risen Lord to come into his life. Immediately he was born again, and his crazy search for life was
ended. Believe it or not, he had found life in the very One from
whom he had been running! And when he received Christ, he
received the strength that he needed to be different.

Is this the end of the story? Not at all. It is just the beginning! The man who was now Onesimus' spiritual father
took his responsibility for the new baby seriously. He fed
him and helped him, encouraged him and advised him. He
gave him plenty to do, and Onesimus rose to the occasion.
Eventually when Paul felt that the time was ripe for Onesimus
to take a deep breath and go home, he found that he didn't
want to part with him. Onesimus had become Paul's right-hand
man!

Paul's sense of humor comes out in the letter of explanation
that he sent with Onesimus to Philemon. He said, "Do you re-

member young 'Profitable' who was a dead loss? He has now become as profitable as his name. He is a tremendous asset to the kingdom. Receive him, and forgive him for my sake. There has been a revolution in the man."

Of course it is only to be expected that there will be a revolution when the risen Lord gets into a person's heart through the new birth. New interests and appetites will be seen. New power and energy will be released. The new birth will change a dead man into a living man who will no longer be a spiritual corpse, but a complete person who has a contribution to make.

Do you feel that you would like to check on your condition? Do you realize how much you need life? Do you know how to find life? Are you prepared to go along with Onesimus? Here is the path that he took. It started with religion without reality that led to rebellion. This made him run and rob. Then came the moment of realization. Repentance and retribution followed. He received Christ, and was revolutionized. Check right now on your position.

Points to Ponder

1. Religion without reality leads to rebellion.
2. Rebellion makes men run.
3. Running from God involves robbing God.
4. Read Malachi chapter one.
5. Realization leads to repentance and retribution.
6. Receiving Christ works a revolution.

A Prayer to Pray

Lord Jesus, I have rebelled and robbed You. I have tried to run from You, but now I realize my sin and Your love. I repent. I'm sorry. Lord Jesus, come into my life by Your Holy Spirit. Give me Yourself, Your life — eternal life. Thank You for hearing and answering this prayer, now I know that I have received you. Amen.

"He that hath the Son hath life" (I John 5:12).

Chapter 5

Then said Martha unto Jesus, Lord, if thou hadst been here, my brother had not died.

But I know, that even now, whatsoever thou wilt ask of God, God will give it thee.

Jesus saith unto her, Thy brother shall rise again.

Martha saith unto him, I know that he shall rise again in the resurrection at the last day.

Jesus said unto her, I am the resurrection, and the life: he that believeth in me, though he were dead, yet shall he live:

And whosoever liveth and believeth in me shall never die. Believest thou this?

She saith unto him, Yea, Lord: I believe that thou art the Christ, the Son of God, which should come into the world.

Jesus said, Take ye away the stone. Martha, the sister of him that was dead, saith unto him, Lord, by this time he stinketh: for he hath been dead four days.

Jesus saith unto her, Said I not unto thee, that, if thou wouldest believe, thou shouldest see the glory of God?

And when he thus had spoken, he cried with a loud voice, Lazarus, come forth.

And he that was dead came forth, bound hand and foot with graveclothes: and his face was bound about with a napkin. Jesus saith unto them, Loose him, and let him go.

John 11:21-27, 39-40, 43-44

5

The Bondage of a Defeated Man

Do you remember our friend Lazarus? The last time we talked about him he was causing quite a sensation. He had just returned from the dead. Sometimes I try to visualize the scene. Martha and Mary, the sisters of Lazarus, were naturally very upset. The crowds were curious. Many of Lazarus' friends were standing around the tomb aimlessly. The cynics were there in force, wondering what Jesus would do now that one of His best friends had died. In the center of the scene stood a large foreboding boulder. It was a great grey symbol of the finality and separation of death itself.

"Roll away the stone," commanded the Master. Shocked exclamations were heard from every side, but none so loud as Martha's, "He's been dead four days; by now he will stink." Martha had a point, of course. But the Lord had talked to her about this. He had said to her, "Thy brother shall rise again." Then He asked her point blank, "Do you really believe that?" and she had said, "Yes." Her difficulty was a common one. She believed in theory that he would rise again eventually, but not that he was going to come out of his tomb once the stone was rolled away. I say this is a common difficulty because much of what we call faith is really nothing more than an intellectual agreement that something might happen. Real faith is more than that! Martha's kind of faith believed that Christ could raise her brother from the dead. The kind of faith that the Lord wants to see doesn't so much believe that He can, but expects that He will. "Roll away the stone." There was a remarkable authority about the words He said, so much so that some did the ridiculous thing — they rolled the stone away. All the darkness of the tomb and the awfulness of corruption was before them. There was a horrified silence. Then the Lord prayed briefly a prayer of thanksgiving. Be very careful that you note the kind of prayer He prayed. "Father, I thank You." Surely one would have expected a prayer something like this, "Oh, Father, I'm in a fix, please help me out of it and do something." Not at all. "Father I thank You," He said loud enough for all to hear. Then, "Lazarus, come forth." I don't know if there was any delay, but I do know that every eye was riveted on the dark entrance to the tomb.

Something stirred. Slowly a white form materialized. It couldn't be! But it was! Lazarus himself moved out into the daylight. The sisters looked at the Lord with utter bewilderment on their faces. The Master had eyes only for the apparition. He didn't get excited over the reappearance of the dead man. Obviously He had something on His mind. But what could possibly be on His mind when He was confronted with a resurrected man? Surely when a man returns from the dead that is all that can be expected! Not by the standards of the Lord. He called out, "Loose him and let him go." No one appears to have noticed that Lazarus was alive but completely bound up with graveclothes. But Jesus noticed.

As soon as the Lord mentioned it, of course, everybody realized Lazarus' predicament. Yards of tight-bound cloth were wrapped around him. His feet were tied together. His hands were fastened to his sides. The whole of his face was covered with a napkin. He was almost unrecognizable as a human being. Lazarus looked more like an animated mummy!

Now of course we cannot possibly overlook the glorious miracle of the new life given to Lazarus, but there is a great lesson for us in this part of the story. It is one thing to recognize the thrill of the new birth, but another thing to know what to do once you have been born again. As Lazarus moved out of his tomb, he must have been very bewildered. Because his feet were tied together he couldn't possibly walk. He probably tried to drag himself along the ground, but that was impossible, too, for his hands were tied. He couldn't even shout for help intelligibly for the napkin filled his mouth. Anyway, his eyes were bandaged so he couldn't see if help was near. Lazarus wasn't dead anymore — but he was sadly defeated.

Let us consider the possibilities of being no longer dead but still defeated. It is by no means uncommon to find born-again Christians who are not really enjoying their Christianity. They know perfectly well that they are born again. In fact, they have testified in many meetings and in a number of situations to the fact of their regeneration. But they also have to admit that while they have no possible cause for complaint about their Lord, they are thoroughly dissatisfied and, in some instances, disillusioned by their own experience of the Christian life. I am sure you have heard people say that the Christian life doesn't work. These people, if they have been born again, are not dead. They are defeated.

Perhaps you may be in this category. Personally I believe that some of the most unhappy people on earth are the defeated Christians. Sometimes they are much more unhappy than people who have never been born into God's family. The reason for this is easy to see. They have enough experience of God to know the reality of His presence and also the possibilities of His power working in their lives. They are, to a certain extent, conscious of the greatness of His promises, but all the while they are confronted with the awful consciousness of their own failure and shortcomings. Because they have received new life, they have discovered new longings and aspirations. Since they started to look into their Bibles they have learned more and more concerning the lives of other Christians and the demands of God upon them. But when they looked into their own lives, they became more and more despondent. If you are in this category, I want you to notice something very important in this story.

The Lord Jesus knew and cared for Lazarus, and He was intensely interested that something should be done for him immediately. It is interesting to note that only the Lord seemed to be concerned about this. Sad to say this is still the case. There are many Christians who get excited about people being converted, but it never seems to concern them that we are not producing the kind of Christians that God wants. They rejoice for a short time over the born-again babies, and then seem almost to lose interest in them. Not the Lord Jesus. He has a great love and concern for His defeated children. So take courage and see what He has in mind for you.

It may be, of course, that you are not too convinced that you are a defeated Christian. You go to church and teach a class or sing in the choir. Maybe you can preach sermons and maybe you have volunteered to be a missionary. All this is wonderful, but, remember, that it is not unusual to find defeated church members, choir singers, preachers and missionaries. You can be engaged in any type of Christian service or worship, and still be as defeated as Lazarus.

It is obvious that great effort, ingenuity and vast amounts of money are being expended on the cause of Christ, but the world is slipping further away from Him regardless of what Christians do. There are, doubtless, many reasons for this, but one of the main reasons is that much Christian activity and service is defeated activity and service. Do we really think the church is working to full capacity? Are we really certain that God is being able to do all that He is capable of doing through His body, the Church? Of course not! I think we ought to ask, "Why is He being hindered and why are we not making the impact that we ought?" It is because much that is being done is being done correctly and carefully, but without any power at all.

Beware of falling into the trap of thinking that because you are quite active you are not defeated. Sometimes the most active are the most defeated! I am sure that Lazarus was extremely active trying to walk and talk and achieve something, but all his activity was thwarted by his graveclothes. The more he struggled, the more frustrated he became. The greater effort he expended, the tighter his bonds gripped him. He wasn't dead though! He was just defeated.

Lazarus gives a marvelous picture of a defeated Christian. As we have already mentioned, he couldn't walk because his feet were tied. He couldn't work either, with his hands tied. Then with his mouth bound up in a napkin he couldn't possibly open his mouth and witness to the power of Christ's working in his life. As far as this man was concerned one word described him. Couldn't! Defeated Christians have the same frustrating experience. They can't walk as they ought in newness of life. The Bible says much about the Christian's walk. The word walk in this sense means a Christian's behavior as he progresses a step at a time through life. One of the things that it says about the Christian's walk is that we should "Walk worthy." In other words, a Christian makes a tremendous claim to be a person who has been born again, a member of God's family, with God's life within him and God's sovereignty ruling over him. Therefore Christians are expected to behave as members of this royal family. Their behavior is expected to match their claim to have God living within them. This is where the difficulty arises so often. It is sadly possible to be a Christian who tries to walk like this and to know that you can't.

This is the experience of a man who is not dead. He is just defeated!

Then there is this dreadful feeling of having your hands tied. I'm sure you have met wonderful Christians who have a great desire to work for God. They have great zeal and willingness, and they say that they must work hard because the "night is coming when no man can work." They recognize the urgency of the situation and long to be thoroughly involved in the work of the Kingdom. Some of them have been so concerned with these things that they have resigned careers and gone into various ministries. Others have been so concerned about youth wandering aimlessly about them that, year after year, they have gone to work with youngsters who have done nothing but abuse their interest. And nothing has happened. They have worked with their hands tied.

Whether it is the natives in the uncompromising jungles or the difficult youngsters in the cities the results have been negligible. Nothing seems to get to the people. They have tried everything, but still they are met with stolid indifference or antagonism, till they have felt like abandoning the project completely. How the Lord loves people who are faithful to the end. He looks at the graveclothes that bind them and cries, "Loose them and let them go!"

Then there is the problem that so many Christians have with witnessing. They are defeated here also. Some know it and admit it causes them great concern. Some know it and won't admit that they are defeated. Instead they make all manner of excuses like, "I'm not gifted that way," or "I witness with my life." Nowhere in the Bible does it say that there is a special gift required to get people talking. In my experience it is obvious that everyone has some degree of natural gift when it comes to talking. All you have to do to check on this point is to raise a subject you know is of interest to the people concerned. Their problem won't be a problem of gift then. It will be a problem of stopping!

If people are interested enough they will talk. Remember the words of Scripture, "Out of the abundance of the heart the mouth speaketh" (Matthew 12:34). Of course, the people who say they witness with their lives are saying something important. But they must remember that a person who witnesses only with his life is a failure. Look what happens when a man witnesses with his life and never opens his mouth. People look at his kind, considerate, friendly life and say, "Isn't he a kind, considerate, friendly man? If everyone was like him the world would be a better place." Are Christians here on earth to make people think what nice people they are? Is the Christian here on earth in these days to make people think that the way to a better world is to have some better people? No, Christians are here on earth to let people know that the only reason for their behavior is that Christ, risen from the dead, is alive in them. They are here to proclaim loud and clear that the only hope for the world is a Christ who alone can save it and make men into new men. But if they never open their mouths to explain this secret, and if they never take the initiative to proclaim their message, they fail! If they accept the acclaim of their fellow citizens, and fail to give God the glory, they are guilty of false pretenses!

I agree that there are many enthusiasts for Christ who are experts at talking and not so good at living. These people are responsible for many others being inoculated against Christ and Christianity for life. Witnessing that ignores living is a pernicious, destructive thing. Living that fails to speak in words that communicate is a frustrating thing. We must face these facts. Many of the people who sit in church these days have nothing to say to others that is worth saying. They are not short of words or subjects, but when they have finished talking they have said nothing. I remember visiting a certain church some years ago. A gentleman who had been given the job of taking care of my needs before the service took me into a small room near the sanctuary. He was embarrassed, but he thought he ought to talk to me, so he took a deep breath and started. He told me about the history of the church, the building problems and the leaky roof. Then he moved on to the organist, the choir and the choir director. This led quite naturally to the minister and his predecessors. On and on he went without daring to stop. Then he gave me a brief account of the history of each family in the church. But gradually he began to run out of material. Naturally, I felt I ought to help so I asked him, "And what about the Lord Jesus?" If I had kicked him he couldn't have looked more startled. He didn't answer me. With a desperate look at his watch he headed for the door muttering, "Come on, it's time to start." He was a man with a life-time of service in that church; his mind was steeped in its traditions and history. His life revolved around its activities, and his mouth spoke out of the abundance of his heart. But his heart had nothing to abound about as far as the Lord was concerned, so his lips were silent concerning Him. The poor, sincere man was defeated because his mouth was all tied up.

Nicodemus had a problem with his witnessing. After his talk with the Lord he went back to his former life and engaged in his normal activities. It is difficult to say if or when he was born again. The fact that he was friendly with Joseph of Arimathaea who was a secret disciple would indicate that perhaps he had trusted the Lord. Also, the way in which he helped with the burial of the Lord after His crucifixion and personally provided all the expensive spices would point to a change of life.

But if he had been born again why did he make such a mess of his opportunities to speak up in the Sanhedrin? One day he had a golden opportunity that no other man ever had. He had the ear of the enemies of the Lord. They respected him and would listen to him. They were actually discussing the Lord in the seat of government and he was free to speak. He rose to his feet and was too diplomatic for words. He simply said, "We can't find a man guilty before he has had a fair trial can we?" He missed his chance. Why couldn't he have told about his personal interview with the Man they were discussing? What was to stop him from outlining the conversation that they had together? Why couldn't he have said something like, "My friends, I know that you have your reservations about this Man, because you feel that He is a political risk and also you believe that He is a blasphemer. If He isn't who He says He is then you are right, but did it occur to you that He might conceivably be who He says He is. Friends and fellow citizens, we need to be very careful on this point. This Man could be the Son of God as He says. He has done some remarkable things as you well know. Don't close your eyes to the facts, men. I have given considerable thought to all He has said and done, and more than that, I ought to tell you that I was so concerned that I actually visited Him at His apartment and heard His side of the story. Gentlemen, He was most convincing. In fact, as a result of my visit with Him and also what has happened in my life since I did what He told me to do, I am convinced that He is none other than the Son of God, the Messiah. Men, I don't expect you all to agree with me, and I don't expect to be the most popular man in the Sanhedrin because of this. But I do want to warn you. You are in danger of making a dreadful mistake!"

History tells of his failure to speak. The merciless blaze of truth shows his failure. We are more fortunate than he because our failure is not in print in the Scriptures, but we are none the less responsible. For we are so often defeated in a witness that could count in lives for all eternity. Do you think that it would be true to say that you are defeated in all or some of these things?

I think that it is important not only to recognize the characteristics of defeat but also the causes. In Lazarus' case it was his graveclothes that kept him bound. His graveclothes were the relics of his deadness. They were absolutely irrelevant to his new life. No one raised from the dead would want to be reminded of death. Yet the tight bandages, weighted down by spices, tainted with corruption and reeking of death, spoke of nothing else. The Lord Jesus demonstrated this for when He rose from the dead He left his graveclothes and His head napkin where they belonged — in the grave. He knew that in His resurrection life graveclothes would be an absolute contradiction. So He came out without them. But Lazarus didn't. He came out with them.

When a man is born again he is regarded by God as a new creation. Old things have passed away, and all things have become new. Now of course it is possible to be a born-again person, but not to live in the enjoyment of everything new. This is because you still want to hang on to the "old things."

A young fellow in Wales once told me that he was having graveclothes trouble. He told me that the relics of his unregenerate days which still bound him were ruining his Christian experience because they had become a vice that he was incapable of overcoming. So, instead of being free and rejoicing in his salvation, he was governed by something that could only mar his testimony and eventually ruin his health. Another young man told me that as a non-Christian he had become so promiscuous that after he was born again he felt a continual hunger for promiscuous activity. But now he hated it and longed to be free. Both these young men, and I could tell you of many more, had found that the things of the old life still had a grip on them after they were born again and that this grip was ruining their spiritual experience and dragging them into defeat. They both discovered also that the Lord could loose them and let them go.

I believe that the Lord intends His children to be set free from all that would hinder and spoil their experience of Him, and I am sure that when people want to be free they can know His ability to release them from their graveclothes.

Are you defeated? Then check on your life and find out what relics of your unregenerate life or natural self are still in control of you. These things are your graveclothes and need to be ripped off. It can be done — and will be done — when you want it. But you need to be in earnest.

Points to Ponder

1. Defeated men can't walk.
2. "I therefore, the prisoner of the Lord, beseech you that ye walk worthy of the vocation wherewith ye are called" (Ephesians 4:1).
3. Defeated men can't work.
4. "We must work the works of him who sent me, while it is day; night comes, when no one can work" (John 9:4 RSV).
5. Defeated men can't witness.
6. "For out of the abundance of the heart the mouth speaketh" (Matthew 12:34).
7. "Therefore, if any man be in Christ, he is a new creature: old things are passed away; behold, all things are become new" (II Corinthians 5:17).

A Prayer to Pray

Dear Lord, I realize that I am no longer dead but in many areas I am defeated. Show me what the graveclothes are and teach me how I can be set free for Jesus' sake. Amen.

Chapter 6

And he said, A certain man had two sons:

And the younger of them said to his father, Father, give me the portion of goods that falleth to me. And he divided unto them his living.

And not many days after the younger son gathered all together, and took his journey into a far country, and there wasted his substance with riotous living.

And when he had spent all, there arose a mighty famine in that land; and he began to be in want.

And he went and joined himself to a citizen of that country; and he sent him into his fields to feed swine.

And he would fain have filled his belly with the husks that the swine did eat: and no man gave unto him.

And when he came to himself, he said, How many hired servants of my father's have bread enough and to spare, and I perish with hunger!

I will arise and go to my father, and will say unto him, Father, I have sinned against heaven, and before thee,

And am no more worthy to be called thy son: make me as one of thy hired servants.

And he arose, and came to his father. But when he was yet a great way off, his father saw him, and had compassion, and ran, and fell on his neck, and kissed him.

And the son said unto him, Father, I have sinned against heaven, and in thy sight, and am no more worthy to be called thy son.

But the father said to his servants, Bring forth the best robe, and put it on him; and put a ring on his hand, and shoes on his feet:

And bring hither the fatted calf, and kill it; and let us eat, and be merry:

For this my son was dead, and is alive again; he was lost, and is found. And they began to be merry.

Luke 15:11-24

6

The Vision of a Defeated Man

THE DEFEATED MAN CAN'T WALK OR WORK OR WITNESS, AS WE saw from the illustration of Lazarus as he came out of his tomb. Instead of walking out in great demonstration of his new life he stumbled and fell. He was tripped by his graveclothes. I want to talk now about another man who had a problem with his graveclothes. I think it would be true to say that his grave- clothes were made of selfishness. His father had great plans for him but he wasn't interested in them. The only thing that con- cerned him was getting what he wanted in life and totally disregarding all other considerations. This is the essence of selfishness. And selfishness always brings a person, whether a Christian or a non-Christian, into defeat.

Many Christians have a gigantic problem with themselves. They are continually conscious of a battle going on within them. One power within them wants to do one thing and another seems to be pulling in the other direction. Part of them has a desire to be what God tells them to be, and the other part won't allow it. Something inside them hates some of the things that they do and wants to stop doing them. Something else inside makes them do the things they hate. They find in them- selves a continual battlefield. It almost seems as if they have a dual personality!

In a way this is exactly what a Christian is. He has two natures or powers within him. One is the tremendous power of self which obviously can only be selfish. The other is the power of the life of the indwelling Lord Jesus through the Holy Spirit. These two powers or natures are in continual conflict. When the power of self is in command then the Christian will reproduce an un-Christ-like selfish life. On the other hand, when the life of the living Lord is being demonstrated this is the result of the power of the Spirit of God being in control.

The young man in our story was a sad picture of a defeated, selfish Christian whose experience we will do well to note. It is always a good thing to be able to learn from other people's mistakes. In fact, that is one reason that the Bible is so careful to record the failures of the Lord's people — in order that we might learn from them.

The story begins with a young man going to his loving father and asking him to give him what he had already been promised. Now there is nothing sinful about that! At first sight it would not appear that he was being particularly selfish. Surely a boy is entitled to go to his father if he needs something, and if his father is a good father he will be delighted to do all he can! True, but this youngster actually had the audacity to suggest to his father that he would like to have his share of what his father was going to leave in his will, and he wanted it immediately. He couldn't wait for his father to die! He needed the money! Did you ever wonder what the father thought? We will never know, but we do know what He did. He granted his son's request.

If there had been any doubt about the caliber of the son when he asked for his inheritance the doubt disappeared the moment he got his hands on the money. Totally regardless of the effect of this action on his father, he packed his belongings and left home, taking his money with him. This was selfishness par excellence.

I am sure that you can see how clear a picture this is of the behavior of a Christian whose life is controlled, not by the gracious Spirit of God but by the merciless dynamic of self. "Heavenly Father, give me this and give me that," is his common prayer. But what is done with what God gives is of tremendous importance. Blessings are not given to Christians by a benevolent God solely that the Christian might be blessed. He intends that the one who has been blessed should use the blessings he has received to be a blessing to others. The Christian who is always getting and never giving is living in the depths of defeat.

Attitude is also very revealing. If a person appreciates what he receives he invariably shows his gratitude in some definite way. If he doesn't then it is certain that he has not been very appreciative. To be the recipient of God's goodness without a corresponding warming and softening to the Lord's wishes and desires is definite evidence of a selfish heart. "God I need You and Your blessing, but I don't want Your plan. So please would You save my soul, forgive my sin and take me to heaven when I die. But Lord, please don't ask me to be what You have already told me You want me to be. I do have my own plans You know." That is the language of a Christian as despicable as the young son in the story. It is the language and attitude of defeat.

It was this blinding attitude on the part of the son that not only made him impervious to his father but also landed him in a far country. He got himself as far away from the influence and the presence of his father as he possibly could. I suppose if he had seen the grief on his father's face even his cold heart might have thawed a little. But he couldn't afford to thaw. His plans were made. If he had seen the development of his father's business, and the responsibilities that were his, he might have experienced some pang of remorse or some slight prick of conscience. But his conscience needed to be chloroformed, and distance was the safest anesthetic. So to the far country he went — out of sight, out of contact, out of reach of all that home and family represented.

When a born-again child struggles with the overpowering selfishness of his own heart, and loses the struggle, the Holy Spirit doesn't leave him. A son can be as bad a reprobate as possible, but he will still be a son. The father might even take the step of disinheriting a disgraceful son, but the son will still have the life of the father within him. The Holy Spirit isn't idle in the heart of the selfish Christian. He is continually speaking and revealing, reminding and suggesting. The selfish saint will do all he can to quiet Him, but to no avail. The conflict of conscience and the awareness of sin from His convictions will reach even into the farthest country.

The greatest desire of the type of Christian about whom we have been talking is to silence the voice of the Spirit. To do this he has to make certain that his mind is busily occupied. He will try to drown the holy voice with other voices which are tuned to the loudest possible volume. He will live as hard and as fast as he is able. He will multiply his interests and activities, and if he really works hard enough, he might even be successful. But what a waste!

The other things that he has to use as an anesthetic will invariably be of secondary importance. (If he is a Christian everything is of secondary importance to Christ.) So he wastes his potential. He doesn't realize it. He misses the point of his life and he fails to be what he was created and redeemed to be. What a waste!

The tragedy is that he will know this deep within. In his quiet moments he will be aware, painfully aware of all that he is missing and his conscience will trouble him. So off he will go again in an ever increasing flurry of escapades and activities. He is caught in a relentless spiral that drags with ever increasing power into a life of utter waste and disgrace.

One day the young son went to his secret hoard for more money and discovered the bags were empty. He had no more money to take. He was broke. It must have been a horrible feeling. He was now far from home, without any real friends, living among strangers who didn't care, out of contact with his father and not a cent to his name. No doubt his mind flashed back to the day he was made rich by his father. He thought again of the sight of his wealth laid in neat piles before him as he counted it and recounted it. The way he'd parted company with his father's hard-earned savings troubled him. The sheer waste and tragedy of his folly swept over him. He was sick at heart.

Then something even worse happened. The Utopia to which he had fled suddenly ceased to be Utopian. The golden city fell on hard times. In the place of well-dressed, well-fed, happy-go-lucky crowds filling the streets, emaciated, pitiful beggars began to appear. They weren't looking for a good time. A good crust would satisfy them. The dreaded famine had arrived. Hunger in its awful intensity gripped the city and desperation filled the hearts of the people. The young man was in a worse state than most. He began to be in need. He needed help financially, medically, physically, socially and above all spiritually. But there was no one to help. The irony of his situation was that he had all the help and love that he could possibly wish for back home, but he didn't want that kind of help. In his heart there was still a stubborn insistence on going his own way, independent of his father, and in this way he continued although the only certainty for him was tragedy.

His heart was no different from any defeated Christian's heart who has a job or work to do and is not prepared to do it. They all go through the same agony of spiritual bankruptcy. They all know the gripping pains of insistent spiritual hunger. Failure and tragedy are no strangers to them, but still they persist in a policy of estrangement from their Heavenly Father.

In pig-headed fashion they drag themselves on to ever increasing chaos and waste, and all the while their Father waits with overwhelming blessing, and possibilities of real fulfillment in His service for them.

Surely most people who see the truth of this in their own lives get back from the far country as quickly as possible and make a new start. The son in the story didn't. He actually went further away. Desperate in his need, he cared not where or how he found help — except, of course, from his father. That was out of the question. So he threw himself on the cold charity of a citizen of the far country. It was obvious that his new employer wasn't remotely interested in him. He was only concerned about getting a man to do a job that no one else was eager to do — feeding pigs. It looks also as if the young man was expected to live with his charges and eat with them. Isn't it an amazing thing to discover how low people can sink?

When you know the perversity of the human heart, including your own, this may not seem so amazing. Children of God are tragically adept at sinking into situations that are obviously fraught with spiritual shipwreck. In fact, it would be true to say that whenever a child of God gets into an attitude of rebellion to his father, and lives in rank selfishness, he is in a vulnerable state. He or she, driven by lack of spiritual reality and hounded by selfish desires, will search hungrily for someone or something to relate to. The realm of relationships with the opposite sex is a common realm of spiritual sinking. So many Christians have sunk to such unbelievable depths because they allowed their desires and hungers to run riot. They have been governed solely by selfish and sensual considerations. The control of the Spirit of God in these matters was neither sought nor found. For many it has meant the end of a ministry. Others have known the heartache of a life that never fulfilled its God-given function. When Christians join themselves to citizens of the far country, and neglect the Father who made them, they ask for trouble and invariably get it.

I have met many of the Lord's people who are perplexed because the Lord has allowed certain things to come into their lives — a divided home — a broken marriage — business failure, and many other things. I believe these things have happened more often than not because the Christians acted in selfish disregard of the Lord's wishes and commands and have reaped what they have sown. It doesn't do any good to ask why God allowed your marriage to be a continual battle if you insisted on marrying someone who wasn't the Lord's. There is no point in blaming God for business failure if your business practice was diametrically opposed to all that the Father desired for the conduct of your business.

Evidently the pigs weren't as hungry as the son, for he was able to get hold of some of their food and steal it from them. Imagine the heir to a fortune stealing a pig's dinner! Perhaps the pigs let him take it because they felt sorry for him! If they did they were certainly kinder than the humans around him, for none of them gave him anything.

There was a turning point in the sad saga of this young man. He had a vision. It wasn't a particularly startling vision. In fact all that happened was that he got an excellent view of himself as he really was. He could have had that vision at any time during his mad career but he didn't, possibly because he was too blinded by other considerations. It is difficult to get a glimpse of one's own spiritual condition when one is wrapped up with all manner of things. In fact, it is usually necessary for a person to come down to the rock bottom of his own self before he can really see himself. His vision wasn't a pretty one. But neither is any vision of self in all its horrid forms. Scene after scene flashed through his mind – his childhood – his father – his brother – his dissatisfaction – his big ideas – his conflict between what was right and what was wrong – his despicable behavior to his father – His wasted opportunity – his sin. All this added together gave this young man his first real glimpse of himself.

Having seen himself he then had to come to terms with himself. It is one thing to see the truth about yourself, but another thing entirely to be prepared to admit it and do something about it.

Have you noticed the striking similarity between the story of Onesimus and this story? On reflection it isn't really surprising. The same power that drove Onesimus, who wasn't a born-again person, was at work in the young son and is still at work in the lives of born-again Christians. Self and sin which ruined Onesimus can still run riot in Christians. Of course Christians have the counteracting dynamic of the living Lord within them, but if they live as if He were not within them they will be guilty of the same sin and selfishness as the non-Christian. This is the reason for much so-called Christian behavior that is sometimes of a lower standard than the behavior of those who don't know the Lord.

A well-disciplined unregenerate person can be more winsome and helpful, kind and considerate than a defeated Christian. Many people are perplexed by this strange fact, but they needn't be. God doesn't eradicate the power of sin when a person is born again. He gives the born-again person the Life that is greater than his sin, but if he refuses to live under the power of that Life he will be a disgrace and a stumblingblock. It is imperative that Christians "come to themselves." There is a great, great need for an awakening of Christian vision — vision of what we really are — vision of what we ought to be — vision of what God will do if we let Him.

Points to Ponder

1. "For the flesh lusteth against the Spirit, and the Spirit against the flesh: and these are contrary the one to the other; so that ye cannot do the things that ye would" (Galatians 5:17).
2. "God, I need You and Your blessing, but I don't want Your plan." This is the language and attitude of defeat.
3. The Holy Spirit isn't idle in the selfish heart of a Christian. He is continually speaking and revealing, reminding and suggesting.
4. Self and sin which ruined Onesimus can still run riot in Christians.

A Prayer to Pray

Lord, help me to see myself as I really am. Give me a vision of my selfishness. Show me the reasons for my defeat. And I will give you the praise through Christ alone. Amen.

Chapter 7

After this there was a feast of the Jews; and Jesus went up to Jerusalem.

Now there is at Jerusalem by the sheep market a pool, which is called in the Hebrew tongue Bethesda, having five porches.

In these lay a great multitude of impotent folk, of blind, halt, withered, waiting for the moving of the water.

For an angel went down at a certain season into the pool, and troubled the water: whosoever then first after the troubling of the water stepped in was made whole of whatsoever disease he had.

And a certain man was there, which had an infirmity thirty and eight years.

When Jesus saw him lie, and knew that he had been now a long time in that case, he saith unto him, Wilt thou be made whole?

The impotent man answered him, Sir, I have no man, when the water is troubled, to put me into the pool: but while I am coming, another steppeth down before me.

Jesus saith unto him, Rise, take up thy bed, and walk.

And immediately the man was made whole, and took up his bed, and walked: and on the same day was the sabbath.

John 5:1-9

7

The Challenge of a Defeated Man

THIRTY-EIGHT YEARS OF LYING ON HIS BACK. THAT WAS THE experience of a man whom the Lord met one day. It was at a place called Bethesda. Many of the unfortunates of Jerusalem used to gather in that place daily. It must have been a depressing place. Crippled people, emaciated and forlorn, huddled in pitiful groups. Beggars were there trying to eke out a miserable pittance. The bitter and the hopeless rubbed shoulders with the weak and dying. There was a continuous hubbub of moans from the suffering, mingled with the shrill cries of the beggars rising higher and higher in an effort to be heard above their fellow-sufferers.

Bethesda means "The House of Mercy," and for this reason the pool of Bethesda is a picture of the place where Christians are to be found — the church. A Christian is a person who knows the difference between justice and mercy. There are many people who feel that the lives they live are up to standard, and they trust that God will do the right thing by them, and treat them fairly in the day of judgment. These people hope for the justice of God. The Bible, however, teaches that the justice of God spells out certain condemnation and eternal separation from God's presence for the lost. This is perfectly just, for God not only gave His law, but He outlined the penalties for failing to keep that law. Justice demands that the right penalty should be passed for the right crime. Anyone who wants justice from God will get it, but it won't be the kind of justice they hope for. Justice means that God metes out to man what he deserves.

Mercy is exactly the opposite. Mercy means that God recognizes our guilt, forgives it for Christ's sake, and then gives us what we don't deserve — new life and rich blessing — the certainty of heaven and the presence of His Holy Spirit. The mercy of God deals with a man in a way he doesn't deserve to be dealt with. Only sinners who repent and claim the effectiveness of Christ's atoning death come into the place called the House of Mercy.

There is a further interesting point about Bethesda. You arrived there by means of the sheep gate. This reminds us of the Lord Jesus who said, "I am the door of the sheep." He insisted on calling people sheep! Sheep are about the most stupid animals on God's earth. They follow each other without thinking. They push their way through hedges built to protect them. They don't seem to be capable of recognizing when they have things provided for them, and they always wander, seemingly aimlessly following the one in front. When you think about it, the Lord knew what He was talking about when He called us sheep!

Human beings tend to act the same way. Of course, when a sheep comes under the control and care of a shepherd, it becomes a totally different animal. It seems to be content and placid. The desire to wander disappears, and the sheep appears to appreciate all the shepherd provides.

Do you remember what the Lord Jesus said about this? He explained that He is not only the Shepherd who organizes the sheep, but He is also the door of the sheep. In other words, He claimed to be not only the source, but also the entrance to all the blessing to be had in the House of Mercy.

Just inside the House of Mercy there was a placid pool. It was calm and still, soothing and peaceful. It was the sort of pool that you can sit by for hours, and let your fears and anxieties sink into its depths. That is exactly what many Christians enjoy about being in the place called Bethesda. They attend the services and enjoy its ministry, and the calmness and stillness of the setting quietens them and fits them for further excursions into the busy world.

Perhaps this is why some churches choose the name Bethesda. Personally, I don't think I would ever be happy choosing that name. I'll tell you why. Bethesda was divided into five compartments, and in these compartments lay many impotent people. Sometimes I feel that this application of the story is a little too true for comfort! The church does tend to be divided on many issues. Obviously, there is much to be said for both sides of most arguments, but I feel that we in the church spend too much time arguing about our different departments, instead of uniting as much as possible against a common foe. I can imagine some of the people who have been lying in their porch for thirty years, refusing to move to another area of the pool, simply because they belong where they are, and no one is going to move them. A few years ago I visited a town in England that possessed five churches, all belonging to the same denomination. Someone suggested that as the average congregation in each church was approximately ten, it would be good to unite. There would have been room for the united congregations to sit comfortably in the choir loft of any one of the churches, but the idea was rejected. Why? Because these people had all been sitting in their porch for so long that they preferred to stay where they were! There are many sad and tragic divisions in the church, but we won't dwell on them.

The posture of the congregation at Bethesda was significant, too. I once had a friend with a remarkable philosophy. He used to say, "Never run if you can walk. Never walk if you can stand. Never stand if you can sit, and never sit if you can lie down." When he was lying down he was happy. Presumably he was happy because lying down is the last word in inactivity. This congregation before us was regular in attendance, but tragically inactive. They lay there and did nothing. I am sure that many recognize this as an amazingly accurate picture of many pew-occupiers. They have entered the place of mercy, but have assumed an attitude of indolence and idleness that is shocking to behold. Why is it that so many of the Lord's people are perfectly happy never to lift a little finger in the Lord's service? Where do they get the idea that they are doing fine as long as they join the congregation around the pool and do nothing?

The description that follows rings a bell. The saints at Bethesda were blind. We usually reserve the idea of blindness for the unconverted, but Paul showed in his letter to the Ephesians that it is not uncommon for converted people to be blind. They need their eyes opened to depths of truth of which they are ignorant. This is the situation in many born-again lives. It may be that you recognize there are vast areas of spiritual understanding that remain dark to you because you are blind. You may admit that you are lame like Lazarus and many of the "halt" congregation at Bethesda, and when you realize that the standard of spiritual development which the Bible talks about is so far from your own condition, you also realize that the description of "withered" fits as well. Blind, halt and withered! What a description of a defeated saint lying by the placid pool.

What can the recumbent saint do? He can wait for something to come from somewhere in some way! There is a wonderful spiritual exercise called "waiting" — "They that wait upon the Lord shall renew their strength. . . ." — but that kind of waiting doesn't mean hopeless inactivity. It means dependence that anticipates blessing. The Bible talks about "waiting for God's Son from heaven." That means an eager looking forward to His return, coupled with a desire to be busy when He comes. That definition hardly fits the congregation at Bethesda!

I think that the worst word used to describe the people in the House of Mercy is the word "impotent." In the Greek it means literally "no dynamic." The sort of dynamic that makes things move is the sheer power of God. This sort of thing is happening in isolated parts of the world, but you know as well as I do that it is not the common thing. The church of God, composed of born-again children of God, is intended to be a living organism that demonstrates nothing less than the overflow of divine power that shows itself in mighty floods of blessing. It isn't happening in many areas because Bethesda is populated with "impotent" folk.

Of course it is easy to be critical, and I have no desire to be offensive or destructive. But I assure you that I am saying this because I believe it, and also because I believe that something can and should be done about it. Impotence and idleness must be exposed. Defeat and death must be recognized.

The Lord moved into Bethesda one day. It is significant that He didn't work on a congregation-wide basis. The contrast between the words "a great multitude" and "a certain man" is startling. If anything is to be done about the Bethesda situation today it will have to be done on the individual level. Congregations are made up entirely of individuals, and the only way in which a congregation can ever be affected is when the individuals are altered. I think that we should always remember this. Next time you feel that the "church" in general is at fault, check to see that the fault is not in you. Churches and congregations are only as strong as the individual members that comprise them. Therefore, the only way to deal with the problems of the whole is to deal with the integral parts of the whole — and that means you and me. Could it be true that your church is what it is because you are what you are? Is it possible that the effectiveness or lack of it in your church is measurable in terms of you multiplied by the total attendance? The Lord wants to deal with the defeated individuals who are responsible for a defeated church. If He isn't allowed to do this by the people concerned, the pool will render value, but the impotent label will still apply.

The account of the Lord's visit says that He saw what was going on. He also knew all about it, and He said something in unmistakable fashion. This is searching truth. You find the same thought in the passages in the Book of Revelation, where the Lord dictated some personal letters to various churches. He explained that He had been watching, that He had evaluated the situation, and that He had something to say. Never forget that He knows better than anyone how defeated you may be. Not only that, but He is adept at evaluating the causes and the consequences of your defeat. He is ready to talk to us about it. His words will be straight to the point as always, and there is no doubt that they will search hearts. However, we need to be ready to expose ourselves to the sharp cutting edge of truth in these days of need. If anything is going to be done to get men and women off their backs and on to their feet, it will be done when recumbent Christians are prepared to listen to what the Master has to say.

I'm sure that the impotent man had been asked many questions during his thirty-eight years by the pool, but the question the Lord asked him was a revelation in itself! "Do you want to be made whole?", He asked. Think about it for a moment! He could have said many different things, but He chose to ask a man who ostensibly could think of nothing else but getting himself cured, "Do you really want to be made fit?" It is common knowledge that it is possible to lose the desire or will to get well after a long illness. Helplessness often leads to hopelessness, and this may be was what the Lord had in mind. Why would a man who spent all his days at the place where he might be made well have got himself into the situation where he might not really want to be made well? I think one reason might lie in the fact that inactivity can become very attractive. Some people discover that the less they do the less they want to do. Maybe he thought, "Now if I say that I would like to be healed, He might heal me. Then I wouldn't be able to lie here any more. I would have to become energetic and busy, and I don't know if I would like that." Or, there is the problem of responsibility. The impotent man had everything done for him. Friends carried him and cared for him. They provided for him, and he enjoyed their goodness. He had no cause to worry, for they did the organizing and the worrying. A man in that condition is in danger of becoming a parasite. His thoughts might have been, "If I get better, then I will no longer be able to let them do everything for me. I might have responsibilities of my own. I don't know if I want to be burdened with responsibility. I must be careful that I don't get healed, and then regret it because of all that I will be expected to do!"

This is the message to defeated saints. "Do you really want to be made powerful and dynamic through the power of God in your life? Or would you much prefer to be able to stay in an unusable condition so that there won't be any risk of being sent to Africa as a missionary? Do you feel that God might put you into a situation that might mean your private life has to be altered so it would be safer to stay defeated, and then there won't be the same risk? Has your evangelical niche become so comfortable or so calm and still and the porch so reassuring and safe that you would not be willing to have the Lord ruffle your water and disturb your defeated calm? Christian, are you really willing to be made whole?"

"It isn't all my fault," you may answer. "If you knew my church and the unfriendly atmosphere, you wouldn't talk like that. You don't know how much we've tried different approaches, and they weren't successful. I don't think you can expect much more than we are doing. When you've said it all you must remember that we are living in days of apostasy. We can't expect too much in these terrible and difficult days."

This sort of answer no more answers the question than the impotent man's answer. He made the same sort of excuses, blaming everyone but himself. He suggested that he had done his best, and that it wasn't his fault that he was still lame and powerless. If the people had been quicker and more helpful, he might have had a different story to tell.

Jesus altered His approach. He ignored the excuses and the moans. He didn't ask any more questions. He spoke with great authority and issued a command — "Stand up, pick up your bed, and start walking." There comes a point in the Lord's dealing with His people when He starts to issue commands.

The Lord's people have great ability in discussing problems, and forming sub-committees to present reports to other committees which will then refer them to another committee for clarification. Then resolutions will be passed, and conferences arranged to discuss the implications of the clarifications of the sub-committee's report to the main committee. I feel that it might be better sometimes if we gave a golden handshake to a few committees, and did what the Lord told us to do!

We must have organization, and we need committees and committee men, but when talking becomes a substitute for obeying, then it is time to realize that to fail to do what the Lord says is disobedience, and disobedience is sin — even if it is dressed up in the orderly cloak of organization. The Lord may cut through our delaying tactics, and give a command, and then the pressure is squarely on us.

The command that He gave seems ludicrous. If the man could walk, he would not have lain there for thirty-eight years. What was the point of telling the man to do something that everyone knew he couldn't do? Had the Lord taken leave of His senses? No, there is a great lesson here for us all.

The Lord never gives a command that we ourselves can fulfill. But He also never commands us to do anything that He Himself cannot perform. He makes available to us all the power of His ability when He commands, so that it is possible for impotent men to reckon with His power at the moment of His command. Then they can obey and do what to them is impossible. This is good news for defeated men, dormant at Bethesda.

With this command ringing in his ears, the invalid had to decide what he was going to do. Obviously he knew that the Lord was capable, and he sensed that He was willing. Therefore the onus was on him to act upon what he knew. The challenge rested squarely on his emaciated shoulders. He decided that he wanted to be different. He chose to allow the Lord to work in his life, knowing full well that all sorts of repercussions would follow. Reckoning with the strength of the Lord Himself, he did what he was told. He stood up. He grabbed his bed roll. He stepped out — straight into trouble. But the person who does what the Lord says, and allows the Lord to conquer his defeat always expects something to happen, and is never disappointed! This is all part of the challenge of a defeated man.

Points to Ponder

1. Why is it that so many of the Lord's people are perfectly happy never to lift a little finger in the Lord's service?
2. The church of God, composed of born-again children of God, is intended to be a living organism that demonstrates nothing less than the overflow of divine power.
3. Churches and congregations are only as strong as the individual members that comprise them.
4. Is your church what it is because you are what you are?
5. Do you really want to be made powerful and dynamic?

A Prayer to Pray

Thank You, Lord, for showing me my own powerlessness. I am sorry about it and admit that I have been self-satisfied and lethargic. Lord, I do want to be what You want me to be for Your sake. Amen.

Chapter 8

And the messengers returned to Jacob, saying, We came to thy brother Esau, and also he cometh to meet thee, and four hundred men with him.

Then Jacob was greatly afraid and distressed: and he divided the people that was with him, and the flocks, and herds, and the camels, into two bands:

And said, If Esau come to the one company, and smite it, then the other company which is left shall escape.

And Jacob said, O God of my father Abraham, and God of my father Isaac, the Lord which saidst unto me, Return unto thy country, and to thy kindred, and I will deal well with thee:

I am not worthy of the least of all the mercies, and of all the truth, which thou hast shewed unto thy servant; for with my staff I passed over this Jordan; and now I am become two bands.

And Jacob was left alone; and there wrestled a man with him until the breaking of the day.

And when he saw that he prevailed not against him, he touched the hollow of his thigh; and the hollow of Jacob's thigh was out of joint, as he wrestled with him.

And he said, Let me go, for the day breaketh. And he said, I will not let thee go, except thou bless me.

And he said unto him, What is thy name? And he said, Jacob.

And he said, Thy name shall be called no more Jacob, but Israel: for as a prince hast thou power with God and with men, and hast prevailed.

And Jacob asked him, and said, Tell me, I pray thee, thy name. And he said, Wherefore is it that thou dost ask after my name? And he blessed him there.

And Jacob called the name of the place Peniel: for I have seen God face to face, and my life is preserved.

And as he passed over Penuel the sun rose upon him, and he halted upon his thigh.

Genesis 32:6-10, 24-31

8

The Surrender of a Defeated Man

JACOB WAS NO STRANGER TO HIMSELF. HE HAD BEEN MADE PAIN-fully aware of his own sinfulness on more than one occasion. His history was one of unfailing defeat. Over the years he had staggered from one crisis to another, and had even perpetrated every dirty trick in the book. No one, not even his own father and brother had been exempt from his sharp practice. He made enemies easier than friends, and he knew that awful experience of having no one to turn to in his hour of need. He was one of the most needy men of his day.

After a long time evading the consequences of his mal-practice, he decided that the time had come for him to "face the music." So he reluctantly gathered together his family and his possessions, and started the long trek home. Wily as ever, he sent scouts on ahead to see what sort of welcome he could expect. Their message didn't help at all. They told him that Esau his brother, looking grim, was marching in their direction with four hundred henchmen, looking equally grim.

Strategy was called for, and as usual Jacob had a plan. He organized a massive present for his brother. More than five hundred and fifty prize animals from his herds were gathered together and driven in the direction of his formidable brother. The herdsman in charge had his instructions to see that Esau had no doubt as to the sender of the present.

Of course Jacob knew that he had cheated his brother out of more than a few hundred animals, and therefore he wouldn't have been surprised if the gift (or bribe) was rejected. So he took further precautions. He divided his considerable wealth into two separated bands, and sent them by separate routes, figuring that if he lost one he could always make do with what was left. He also worked the same principle with his wives, women-ser-vants and sons.

Then, having taken all the precautions that he could to protect his own skin and his own wealth, he settled down for the night. That is, he tried to settle down! One would have thought that he would have had no sleep that night for worrying about his wives wandering defenseless into the path of his furious brother. It is reasonable to assume that the thought of his eleven young sons out in the cold dark night would have kept him awake. But there is no evidence that this was the case. Jacob was as safe as he could be — but he didn't sleep. He had a visitor.

Before we think about the visitor, let us spend a moment looking at Jacob as he sat alone in the dark. His thoughts troubled him. As he looked into the future he was quite understandably afraid. There didn't seem to be much hope for him. Of course he had no one to blame but himself, but that didn't make him any the less afraid.

Then he had time to reflect. As he looked back over his life he thought of the tremendous advantages he had enjoyed. The blessings that God had sent his way came before him. Like a drowning man he saw his past life flashing before his eyes. And he was ashamed. He knew that he had squandered his advantages and abused his blessings.

Men have a habit of becoming reflective when they are left alone in the stillness. They tend to become almost melancholic when they sit down and think. That is why they don't like to be left alone with their thoughts. They switch on a radio the moment they enter a room or drive off in their car. The television is indispensable when they have an idle moment. If neither is available, and friendly company is not on hand, they stick their heads in a book. But they hate to be left alone with their thoughts because their thoughts often trouble them.

Jacob was in this frame of mind when his unexpected visitor arrived. The Lord Himself visited Jacob in that lonely place. Be careful to note the position. He was afraid of the future, ashamed of the past, and alone. Then the Lord arrived. We are not told how the interview started, but we do know that it developed into a wrestling match. It takes two to make a fight, and so while the Bible says that the Lord wrestled with Jacob all night, it is obvious that He wrestled because Jacob resisted.

This is a most remarkable thing! Imagine Jacob in that sort of a situation wrestling with God. He was not wrestling with God to try to squeeze some blessing out of Him, but wrestling because he was resisting God with all his strength. He had absolutely nothing to lose by surrendering to God, and he had everything to gain. What could be worse than his situation at that moment? His past was a disgrace. His prospects were gloomy to say the least. His heart was gripped by an awful sense of loss and shame. He had a golden opportunity to put things right with his God, who had taken the trouble to visit him personally.

There was no one around to hinder. He could never wish for more ideal circumstances to have dealings with the Lord. The Lord was anxious to help and to bless. And all Jacob could do was fight. He fought God that night as hard as he could. The battle went on all night. While we must see the folly of Jacob's stupidity, we must also admit that it takes quite a man to wrestle with God through a cold, dark night!

The man who resists God knows the coldness and darkness of his spiritual night as no other man knows. Nothing seems to make sense. Nothing satisfies. Everything appears hopeless and the more he struggles the worse everything becomes. But still he wrestles.

It is quite a few years since I did any wrestling, but I can still remember the basics. There are many different styles, of course, but the main idea is to get the opponent on the floor and keep him there. I suppose that is the position of defeat — flat on the canvas unable to move. The difficulty comes from the fact that your opponent not only wishes to make sure that you are unsuccessful in your attempt but he also insists on trying to put you on your back! So you have the strange situation of two people trying to do the same thing to each other while they are both trying to stop the other from doing it! Complicated? Yes, but great fun if it is only sport. Of course there was no entertainment value in what Jacob was doing. He was trying to stop God from having supremacy over him and he was trying to gain the advantage over God. This was stark lunacy, but he fought on.

The apparent stalemate is only resolved when one is able to outwit the other or to overcome him with superior strength. Obviously God could have slapped Jacob down at any moment He wished, but He was gracious enough to give Jacob the chance to submit of his own free will. This is always God's way of dealing with man. He could obliterate man at any given moment, but if He did He would defeat His own ends. He wants the glad submission of His subjects, not the unwilling capitulation of rebellious serfs.

Wrestlers have to move and think quickly. They need to be able to recognize an attack, resist it, and turn it to their advantage all in one fleeting moment. They get a hold on the opponent's head. He obviously doesn't like it, and resists by putting a merciless hold on the other wrestler's arm. No one likes anything by this time, so one trips the other. But at the moment of the trip, as they are both in midair one twists the other underneath and wins the fight.

In His dealings with Jacob God switched His point of attack continually. He got a grip on Jacob's sin and said, "Jacob submit." He got hard unrelenting resistance. So He left His hold and switched to Jacob's past. "Admit your failure," He said, but resistance was the only response. And so on He wrestled, graciously, persistently straining to bring his rebellious child to the point where He could do something with him — the point of submission.

As the dawn began to break at the close of that dark night, God came to the reluctant conclusion that He was getting nowhere with Jacob. This is one of the most fearful things that I have read concerning God's dealings with man. To think that God can be thwarted so long and so violently that He decides that there is nothing to be done about the person He is longing to win! I believe that it is possible for a child of God to be so persistent in his rebellion that God decides not to struggle anymore. In a sense it is as if God says, "All right, you have shown Me quite clearly that you will not accept My plan and acknowledge My Lordship. You obviously want to go your own way, so I will let you have your will." This may sound like victory for man over God, but it isn't. It is God graciously allowing man the right to exercise his own will and have his own way. God isn't the loser, but man certainly is!

When the divine Wrestler came to this conclusion He touched the hollow of Jacob's thigh and dislocated it. I am sure that Jacob immediately lost all interest in wrestling! The dislocation of the smallest member of the body can cause excruciating pain, but the agony of a dislocated thigh must have been unbearable. The proud wrestler couldn't lie down quick enough! He was beaten and he knew it. Of course God could have started in this way. He could have moved straight into battle and put Jacob down in one easy movement. But He chose not to do it that way. The Lord is always much happier when His child submits voluntarily rather than under compulsion. Obviously the willing surrender brings more joy to the heart of the child of God too.

Whenever Jacob looked back to the night of his fight he would always be reminded that he gave in to God because he had to and not because he wanted to. This would color his attitude for the rest of his days. God still has to act in this kind of fashion. If a Christian insists upon being useless to God then God in all probability will feel it necessary to place the rebellious one in such a position that he will not get in God's way. He may have to put him off to one side, where he will cause the least possible trouble. This does not mean, however, that he loses his salvation. Service is the point of consideration here, not salvation. His salvation is secure, but his service will be null and void. You can see the thing that God has in mind in the letters that the Lord wrote to the churches in the Book of Revelation. He said that it might be necessary to remove the Candlestick, meaning that He would terminate the effectiveness of the church's ministry and witness. Incidentally, if you look for those churches today you will have difficulty finding them. It would appear that the Lord was forced to do what He said He might have to do.

Then the silence of the night was broken by some ghastly words, "Let me go." It wasn't the rebellious Jacob who said that. It was the Lord who spoke. He had gone as far as He could with Jacob and He was prepared to move into other lives that might prove more willing and amenable to His desires. "Jacob let me go, I am moving on. You have been struggling all these years. Now you can have what you wish — complete freedom to go your own way."

The words bit deep. Jacob was suddenly confronted with the possibility of being given what he wanted. The right to determine his own destiny for which he had fought so long, was his. And he didn't want it. Do you think that he was being capricious? Was he always changing his mind and never knowing what he wanted? No, that wasn't his trouble. He realized in a flash how much he needed the Lord and how hollow everything would be without Him.

His answer revealed his true thoughts. "I will not let you go except you bless me!" Jacob had a great need of blessing in his life and he knew it. Also, he was fully aware that the only

One who could make real the blessing he needed was the One who was about to leave him to his own wilfull stupidity. Now he was desperate. There was nothing that he wanted more than the fullness of God's blessing on his life. The transition couldn't have been greater, and it couldn't have come quicker. In a twinkling of an eye his heart was changed.

There is no deliverance from defeat and no fullness of blessing for the rebellious and the halfhearted. Those who hunger and thirst after righteousness are the ones who are filled. It is the thirsty who come to Christ and drink of Him who see the rivers of living water flowing from their lives. There is nothing superlative about the Christianity of the wavering, half-hearted, divided saint. There is only defeat, heartbreak, barrenness and regret. But Jacob was different now. He longed for all that God had for him. The reason he changed his mind was that he realized he was useless. He was crippled and alone. He was vulnerable and defeated. He was friendless and aimless. He was consumed now with the emptiness of his spiritual condition, and it all came about through a dislocated thigh.

No doubt you know of instances in the lives of Christians similar to this. Perhaps they have been confronted with some tremendous challenge, striken with some overwhelming sorrow or crippled by some disease. It may be that they have gone gaily along their barren pathway for years and it was only when they were put on their backs and shown in no uncertain terms the uselessness of their lives that they faced up to reality. If you know people like this, and you also know that as a result they became desperate for the blessing of God in overflowing measure in their lives, you are fully aware that they wouldn't have missed the experience for all that man could offer them. They will testify to the fact that the blessing resulting from their sorrow, disappointment or disability made everything worthwhile.

Have you come to the point of surrender either through the pressure of circumstances or through a heart that is hungry for God? Have you laid hold of God with all the intensity of your being and said, "God, I'm desperate for you and your best, and I will settle for nothing less." This is the pathway out of defeat.

But the Lord hadn't finished with Jacob. "What's your name?" He asked. Strange words indeed! Surely the Lord knew. Anyway it was hardly the time for introductions! Quietly came the answer, "Jacob." The answer was more than just an acknowledgment of name. It was an acknowledgment of character. It was a confession. " 'Twister,' that's my name. 'Contriver and Cheat' is my name, 'Warped and Corrupt,' I am called." Jacob was actually telling the Lord, with deep contrition, what he really was. And that was music to the ears of God. Did you know that one of the things that the Lord loves to hear is the full and frank confession of our lips? Are you aware that the Lord longs for you to come to the point of admitting what you are? Has He heard it from your lips?

Listen to the thrilling response of the Lord, "You are no longer Twister; you are now Prince of God." Then the Lord gave His reasons for the change of name. "You have power with God and you will have power with men, Israel. You couldn't possibly be called Twister when you are going to be the sort of man who can be the means of the power of God being released among men. You have prevailed, Israel. Through admitting defeat you have gained the victory and you are going to be triumphant. Twister isn't the name for that kind of man."

What exciting words and what thrilling prospects for Israel! But this is the sort of exciting thing that God loves to do. He specializes in this kind of transformation. This is exactly the kind of miracle He plans for you. Let me remind you when it came about and how it came about. It all started when Jacob surrendered unconditionally to the Lord. Then his heart attitude changed. Instead of defiance to God it became reliance upon God. His resistance became dependence. God can and will make any Twister into a prince when the Twister is hungry to be different — hungry enough to agree to the totalitarian control of his God upon his life. Then the twisted one must realize that utter dependence upon his Lord assures full supply of all his needs. This attitude allows the Lord to move into business.

Of course, that isn't the end of the story. It really begins there. Israel named the place to remind him of the fact that he had met God face to face. It became holy ground to him. But that wasn't his only reminder. He had the other reminder with him for the rest of his days — he limped on the leg that had been dislocated. From that day on he never took a step without the evidence of his surrender that led to victory. I can imagine him saying, as he went down on one leg, "That reminds me of the day I was put on my back." Then, as he inevitably rose on his other leg, he thought, "Praise the Lord for He raised me up and made me walk in a new way."

Limping Israel went on his way and the sun rose upon him. There is something lovely and fresh about the sunrise, but it is nothing compared to the radiance that envelops a life abandoned to God and dependent upon Him.

Have you been through what Jacob went through?

Points to Ponder

1. "And Jacob was left alone; and there wrestled a man with him until the breaking of the day" (Genesis 32:24).
2. "I am not worthy of the least of all the mercies, and of all the truth, which thou hast shewed unto thy servant" (Genesis 32:10).
3. Jacob had absolutely nothing to lose by surrendering to God, and he had everything to gain.
4. "Remember therefore from whence thou art fallen, and repent, and do the first works; or else I will come unto thee quickly, and I will remove thy candlestick out of his place, except thou repent" (Revelation 2:5).
5. "Blessed are they which do hunger and thirst after righteousness: for they shall be filled" (Matthew 5:6).
6. "In the last day, that great day of the feast, Jesus stood and cried, saying, If any man thirst, let him come unto me, and drink. He that believeth on me, as the scripture hath said, out of his belly shall flow rivers of living water" (John 7:37, 38).

A Prayer to Pray

Lord, I admit that I have been defying You rather than relying upon You. Like Jacob I have fought You, and I am sorry. Lord, I am hungry for You and Your blessing. Make me a prince, through Jesus Christ alone. Amen.

Chapter 9

Then they took away the stone from the place where the dead was laid. And Jesus lifted up his eyes, and said, Father, I thank thee that thou hast heard me.

And I knew that thou hearest me always: but because of the people which stand by I said it, that they may believe that thou hast sent me.

And when he thus had spoken, he cried with a loud voice, Lazarus, come forth.

And he that was dead came forth, bound hand and foot with graveclothes: and his face was bound about with a napkin. Jesus saith unto them, Loose him, and let him go.

Then many of the Jews which came to Mary, and had seen the things which Jesus did, believed on him.

But some of them went their ways to the Pharisees, and told them what things Jesus had done.

Then gathered the chief priests and the Pharisees a council, and said, What do we? for this man doeth many miracles.

If we let him thus alone, all men will believe on him: and the Romans shall come and take away both our place and nation.

But the chief priests consulted that they might put Lazarus also to death;

Because that by reason of him many of the Jews went away, and believed on Jesus.

John 11:41-48, 12:10, 11

9

The Making of a Dangerous Man

WE HAVE ALREADY SEEN LAZARUS IN TWO DIFFERENT CONDITIONS. Originally we met him in his tomb where he was a picture of a spiritually dead man. Then he met with the One who calls Himself "The Resurrection and the Life," responded to His call, and came forth from his tomb. He was born again! But all was not well with Lazarus. He was all bound up with the relics of his death. His new life was thwarted by clinging, binding bandages.

He had new life in exchange for death, but he was horribly defeated. This, as we have seen, can be the experience of those who have been born again. They aren't dead, but they are defeated. Has the Lord anything to offer to defeated saints? Or is defeat the normal experience of those who come to newness of life in Christ?

The answer comes loud and clear in the great shout of the Lord outside Lazarus' tomb — "Loose him and let him go." The Lord does not intend that those who are born again should spend the rest of their days on earth bound and gagged, defeated and disillusioned. He has plans laid for the redeemed that will enable them to live life in the liberty that He gives. His idea for the born-again children of God is that they should thoroughly enjoy their salvation. It is not that they should spend their time on earth longing to get away from it, because it has them beaten, but they should thoroughly revel in the life that He gives on earth while they are making their journey toward heaven and its eternal glory. I believe that the great cry of the Risen Lord today is "Loose him and let him go."

I am certain that no one had to tell Lazarus that he was frustrated. His bondage was obvious to him, and to everybody else. This is a rather sobering thought. When a man is bound and beaten it is perfectly obvious to the onlookers. This is something that the church needs to recognize. People, for all their cynicism, are watching the Christians. They profess to be disinterested, but under cover of these protestations, they keep a keen eye on what the Christians are doing. One day I asked a young Englishman, "Do you ever go to church?" He looked at me in amazement and said, "You must be joking!" "No," I replied, "I am perfectly serious." His reply was shattering. "Look mate," he said, "I'm miserable enough. I don't want their misery. I have enough problems of my own without any more."

Then he told me how he had stood outside a church on Sunday mornings watching the people go in, and waiting for them to come out. He added, "You want to know something? They looked as miserable when they came out as when they went in."

Now, I am perfectly well aware that it is easy to be critical, but I think that this young man had a point. He watched and he evaluated on the basis of what he saw. He saw nothing that impressed him. Perhaps he saw what the people outside Lazarus' tomb saw! Both he and they recognized defeated men when they saw them.

There is nothing that binds the life of a Christian which the Lord Jesus cannot overpower. There are no such things as graveclothes that He cannot tear away. Once the Lord has been given the opportunity to do all that He can do with the Christian who is having trouble, there is no limit to what He will do. But first He must have a willing, submissive person, who is ready for anything that the Lord proposes to do.

Some graveclothes cling tightly. There are gravecloth relationships that bind and blight and yet are tremendously attractive to the one who is bound. There is no liberty for the person who finds the graveclothes more attractive than the Lord. No released life will ever be enjoyed by a person content with bondage and unconcerned with the life that Christ intends to live in them. Desire and aspiration play a tremendous part in the life of the person whom the Lord will set free.

Some graveclothes appear to be so strong that people who long to be rid of them fear that it is an impossible thing to hope for. They are convinced of the mighty power of the Lord to do great things in a general sort of way, but they have absolutely no expectation that He will do anything with their problem.

Take the graveclothes of temperament, for example. Some

people bound by and to a bad temper are terribly conscious of what they are, and what they do. Often they get sick at heart after an outburst that they could not control. But instead of letting the Lord do something, they try to excuse themselves with such inanities as, "Well, I suppose it's my nature, and I'll just have to learn to live with it. You·must remember, of course, that my grandfather had a bad temper, and my Aunt Agatha had red hair, so what hope is there for me?" There is every hope for them, if they will come to terms with the words of the Lord!

How does it work? This is the question that we are all bound to ask in these circumstances. The answer is found in the words of Paul to the Roman Christians. "The law of the Spirit of life in Christ Jesus has made me free from the law of sin and death" (Romans 8:2). This may require a little explanation. The law of the Spirit of life is the principle of the Spirit who makes the life of the risen Christ real in the lives of all those who receive Christ. When Nicodemus was born again, he was born of the Spirit. In other words, the new life that he received came through the entrance and invasion of his spirit by the Holy Spirit. So then, at the moment of his conversion, he was exposed to the possibility of a new principle of life — the principle of the mighty Holy Spirit working in his life overcoming the power of sin.

The old power of sin and self uncontrolled can only lead a Christian into defeat, but when the Holy Spirit is allowed to be the power that He undoubtedly is, in a believers' life, the sheer dynamic of His life can and does overcome. In this way there is deliverance from bondage. Only in this way is it possible for the Lord to say, "Loose him and let him go." Did you know this? Have you a burning desire to be released from the sin that binds you and the habits and failings that trouble you? Do you believe that the Lord can handle the problem? Then you must speak to the One who lives within you by His Spirit, and ask Him to set you free. But you need to ask in a special way! You know as well as I do that it is possible to ask God to do things, and never to expect anything to happen. It is useless asking God in this way. You must ask Him to do what He has promised to do, stating the promise and then thanking Him that He will.

I well remember a young man who was a member of a group that my wife and I took to Holland for a conference. He had a problem with smoking. Every evening he used to go alone to a quiet canal for his evening cigarette. The boy was absolutely addicted, and had been since he was about twelve years old. In fact he smoked so heavily that he had to manufacture his own supplies! One night I talked to the group about the words of the Lord Jesus when He stated, "Ye shall know the truth, and the truth shall make you free" (John 8:32). Then I showed that when the Lord said the truth would do the emancipating, He was referring to Himself, for He added, "If the Son therefore shall make you free, ye shall be free indeed" (John 8:36). Obviously He was using the term "Truth" as a description of Himself. I tried to show the young people that whatever it was that was binding them in their Christian experience, the Lord through His indwelling life could, and would, set them free.

Unknown to me, there was a hungry boy listening. He was hungry to be rid of the habit that was his master. He heard that a Christian is a person who has a power greater than any other power within him. Therefore he knew that for him to claim to be a Christian, but at the same time to be living dominated by a lesser power than the Spirit of God was a contradiction. So he evaluated his graveclothes, and knew that they had to go.

As usual, he went down to the canal. But for the first time he went there longing to be set free. He did an unusual thing. He took out his cigarettes, and threw them into the canal, one at a time. As each cigarette fell into the water he repeated the words that he believed with all his heart. "If the Son therefore shall make you free, ye shall be free indeed." He testifies to this day that the Lord had the victory over this thing.

Naturally he had many battles over this problem. Many were the times that he longed for a calming, soothing smoke. The Lord hadn't taken away his desire and the Lord hadn't given him a new strength of will power. Every time he claimed the promise of God, and each time he reckoned on the adequacy of His Lord he was loosed.

I am not, of course, suggesting that smoking is a heinous sin. But in all fairness I would say that I don't like the habit, and that when a Christian is in bondage to it he is living a contradiction. I am simply using this as an illustration of the possibilities and also the means of liberty being experience in the place of bondage. Perhaps you have never smoked in your life. All right, this isn't your problem, but something is. What is it? I don't know, but I do know that the Lord says to you "Loose him." Is that what you want?

I am so glad that the Lord Jesus added, ". . . and let him go." These words hold a tremendously exciting thought for me. I would like to share it with you. Have you ever fired an arrow from a bow? What do you do? The first thing you do is to load the bow with the arrow. Then the string must be drawn back until the tip of the arrow reaches the front of the bow. Then you simply loose it. What do you do next? Drop the bow and run after the arrow pushing it? Do you try to keep up with it so that you can encourage it? No, of course not! You loose it, and you let it go.

You see, the moment that you loose the arrow the power that is linked to it automatically takes over. It does it with such enthusiasm that the arrow defies other forces, and speeds with tremendous velocity toward its target. The moment of release is the moment of new momentum. Listen again to what the Lord said, "Loose him and let him go." And this is exactly what happened.

Lazarus had a fantastic power within him. It was the power of a resurrection life given to him by the Lord Jesus. This life had not been allowed to express itself until the moment of release. But once released, that was it! All that the new life had been waiting for was a chance to get moving. And when the chance came the chance was taken. Lazarus really began to go!

You are in a similar position. The moment you claim release from your bondage through the work of the Spirit within you, the dynamic of this same Spirit is ready to propel you in a new path of triumph and victory. Christians don't need more power to "go" in their Christian lives. They need to have graveclothes removed and to reckon with the power within them. They need nothing less than the power of the resurrection life of the Lord Himself.

Isn't it a tragedy that there are so many Christians who have never realized that they have within them all the thrilling power of the risen Lord? It is obvious to me that there is only one person who would want to hide this from the Christian's eyes. It is the devil himself. He knows that once Christians find out about this they will really get moving. When the indwelling life within them is released, he will be in for real trouble. So he blinds people's eyes. He persuades Christians that graveclothes are normal. He tells them that they are doing quite well even though everyone else knows that they are falling around gagged like Lazarus. This is one of the masterpieces of deceit. Has he deceived you?

Immediately, things began to happen. The released man stepped out with a smile on his face and a glint in his eye. He had tasted death and he knew what life was. He had seen the reality of the after life, and he could see the bewilderment of those still on earth. Now he was familiar with the facts of the things confronting every man, and he knew the remedy. He could not rest until he had shared what he had discovered.

I have met so many men of God who spend all their time trying to instill some sense of burden into the people in their charge. They use all manner of methods to try to stimulate enthusiasm. But they admit failure. Mission secretaries tell stories of needs that are not being met. Veteran missionaries speak of no one to replace them when they retire. What happened to the concern and the burden that used to be talked about?

I am not sure what happened, but I know how it can be remedied. Show a man or a woman, boy or girl the possibilities of the risen Lord cutting loose in their lives. Enable them to come to terms with Him. Then move smartly out of their way! For when a man is loosed he'll go. You won't have to manufacture burden or produce concern. When the Lord is moving in a man there will be no lack of either burden or concern. Nor will there be a shortage of power.

So great was the impact of Lazarus that the crowds began to congregate. They wanted to see the reality of this new life with their own eyes. Anxious people gathered around him to hear him speak of his experiences. Crowds of seeking people came to him to be shown how they could experience the reality of the Lord in their lives. Many people were turned into the kingdom. The Lord was in business in no uncertain fashion.

There is something thrilling and exciting about a person who is caught up in the full flow of the life of the Spirit. Things happen and continue to happen. Many predictable things result, and the most unpredictable too. People begin to be drawn to the one who so obviously demonstrates the blessing of God. Hungry souls congregate and the angels rejoice. There is joy in heaven and blessing on earth when men and women are loosed and let go.

But don't think that it is all honey! When the Lord gets busy His enemy does too! Satan has nothing to fear from defeated Christians. In fact he is rather fond of them. They cause him no concern, and they give people plenty of arguments against their Christianity. He doesn't lose any sleep when defeated saints play right into his hands. But if they once get moving, so does he! And that spells trouble for them.

The stir caused by Lazarus was so great that the chief priests got their heads together, and believe it or not they plotted to put Lazarus to death. Poor old Lazarus had only just got himself resurrected, and they wanted to put him back in his tomb! This must be one of the dirtiest plots of all time!

Why did they take him so seriously? Because he was turning people from darkness to light, and from the power of Satan to God. He had to be exterminated because he was dangerous. He wasn't dead any more. And he wasn't defeated. He was dangerous!

Paul talked about three classes of people recognized by God. He called them natural, carnal and spiritual men. Here we have the same picture. Natural men are dead. The carnal are defeated. And spiritual men are dangerous. I believe that there are only three kinds of people in God's economy – the dead, the defeated, and the dangerous. You may feel that you aren't defeated, but you know that you aren't causing the devil any loss of sleep. Sorry, if you aren't dangerous you are defeated. But you may say, "We can't all be dangerous in the forefront of the battle." I can't think why. You live among people, don't you? They need a glimpse of reality, don't they? The risen Lord lives in you by His Spirit, doesn't He? The promises of God apply to you, don't they? Then don't make excuses. If you aren't dangerous with all these opportunities, then you are defeated. But remember the words of the Lord that make the defeated dangerous –"Loose him and let him go."

Points to Ponder

1. "Loose him and let him go."
2. "And ye shall know the truth, and the truth shall make you free" (John 8:32).
3. "If the Son therefore shall make you free, ye shall be free indeed" (John 8:36).
4. "When a man is loosed, he'll go."
5. "When the Lord gets busy His enemy does too!"
6. If you aren't dangerous you are defeated.

A Prayer to Pray

Lord, I don't think the devil has lost any sleep because of me, but I want things to be different. By Your Spirit set me free from my graveclothes, and make me dangerous for the sake of Jesus Christ. Amen.

Chapter 10

And in those days, when the number of the disciples was multiplied, there arose a murmuring of the Grecians against the Hebrews, because their widows were neglected in the daily ministration.

Then the twelve called the multitude of the disciples unto them, and said, It is not reason that we should leave the word of God, and serve tables.

Wherefore, brethren, look ye out among you seven men of honest report, full of the Holy Ghost and wisdom, whom we may appoint over this business.

But we will give ourselves continually to prayer, and to the ministry of the word.

And the saying pleased the whole multitude: and they chose Stephen, a man full of faith and of the Holy Ghost, and Philip, and Prochorus, and Nicanor, and Timon, and Parmenas, and Nicolas a proselyte of Antioch:

Whom they set before the apostles: and when they had prayed, they laid their hands on them.

And the word of God increased; and the number of the disciples multiplied in Jerusalem greatly; and a great company of the priests were obedient to the faith.

And Stephen, full of faith and power, did great wonders and miracles among the people.

Then there arose certain of the synagogue, which is called the synagogue of the Libertines, and Cyrenians, and Alexandrians, and of them of Cilicia and of Asia, disputing with Stephen.

And they were not able to resist the wisdom and the spirit by which he spake.

Then they suborned men, which said, We have heard him speak blasphemous words against Moses, and against God.

And they stirred up the people, and the elders, and the scribes, and came upon him, and caught him, and brought him to the council,

And set up false witnesses, which said, This man ceaseth not to speak blasphemous words against this holy place, and the law:

For we have heard him say, that this Jesus of Nazareth shall destroy this place, and shall change the customs which Moses delivered us.

And all that sat in the council, looking steadfastly on him, saw his face as it had been the face of an angel.

Acts 6:1-15

10

The Impact of a Dangerous Man

LAZARUS WASN'T THE ONLY ONE WHOSE NAME FIGURED PROMI-
nently on the devil's blacklist. In fact, in the early days of the
church there seems to have been an abundance of dangerous
men. We have no record as to whether Lazarus was put to
death by his enemies, but we do know about Stephen.

I must admit that I feel that Stephen's story is one of the
most exhilarating that I have ever read anywhere. No tale of
fiction can match this story for action and color. I have yet
to find a story that has greater suspense and which records
more manly courage than this one. But I think the main reason
that I like it so much is the challenge it brings to my own heart.

Let us spend a few moments learning from Stephen — the
man who was so dangerous that the devil had him put away
as soon as he got into his stride. It is important to note that
Stephen was not an apostle. His ministry was not specifically
preaching and praying. Stephen was appointed by the early
church to be a Christian businessman. (Personally I think
that he ought to be patron saint of CBMC!) It was like this:

There was a certain amount of welfare work to be done in
the early church. People began to complain that they were
being overlooked, and that they were not getting their share
while others seemed to be getting preferential treatment. Evidently the apostles had more work than they could handle, and
so they decided to appoint some men who could look after
the business affairs of the church while they concentrated on
the spiritual matters. Stephen was the first man appointed
under this scheme.

I feel that there are important issues involved in this turn
of events. No doubt you will agree with me that we, the church,
are not making a very great success of evangelizing the world.
On many fronts we are retreating instead of advancing. In
numerous countries, including my own, the church has lost her

grip on the people, and has become so remote that most people disregard her unless they want a white wedding or a socialite christening, or a decent burial.

While there are wonderful saints of God scattered far and wide in distant and often dangerous lands, we cannot help knowing that on the whole the supply of missionary candidates is drying up. The support for these fine people is not always forthcoming, and they are constantly hampered through shortage of funds and equipment. The picture is not too encouraging!

In the land where the Gospel appears to be spreading more rapidly than any other, namely Brazil, the situation is not all rosy. For even in Brazil there are more people being born every day than are being born again. You don't need to have a degree in mathematics to see that the Gospel is losing ground there. Now, if it is true that even where we are most effective we are still losing ground, what does it mean? I believe it means that we desperately need a mighty movement of God in our people reaching out to the uttermost parts of the earth. But where are the people? They are sitting in churches on Sunday, and sitting behind desks on Monday. Some of them attend Sunday school on the first day of the week, and live on campus every other day of the week. Others work in the womens' class on the Lord's Day, and labor in their homes every other day. In short, there is no real shortage of people to do the job, for the people who know the Lord are to be found in all walks of life, in every stratum of society, in thousands of geographical locations.

The businessmen and women are the people who need a vision of how dangerous they can and ought to be in their secular lives. It is my firm conviction that we must work in these days for nothing less than the total mobilization of the total congregation. At the moment we have the ludicrous situation of one or two men doing a work that it is humanly impossible to accomplish, while hundreds of others are busy making money. It is the people in the pew who hold the answer to the problem of getting the message to the people.

Personally I feel that our major need is not more men in the pulpit, but more men and women, dangerous of course, moving out from their pews. Let us pause for a moment at this point.

How many people regularly attend your place of worship?

How many areas do they represent? How many people do they touch in their working week? How many others do they contact in their social life? How many homes are within the vicinity of homes represented in your congregation? If you take time to count all these contacts I am certain you will get a surprise. There is a ready-made mission field already in easy reach of your church. Mobilized properly, your church congregation could see mighty victories for God and resounding defeat for the old serpent.

We must assume, of course, that the businessmen and women, the students and the school children know what it is to be loosed and let go. Seldom do I ever face a congregation of the Lord's people so neat and spruce on a Sunday morning without thinking of the untold and unknown potential wrapped up in them. Very rarely do I ever fail to be thrilled at the possibilities latent in a well-dressed, well-mannered, well-educated congregation, when I think of where they will be on the Monday morning. I am sold on the conviction that there is yet time to get the message with which we have been entrusted to the people who need it most. But it will only be done through dangerous businessmen and women. We need the Stephens.

There are three aspects of Stephen's life that I think are of value to us. His life was irreproachable. There is no substitute for a life of consistency and conviction. The dangerous Christian is always a Christian who lives his Christianity in the eyes of men and women in such a way that they know exactly by watching him, what he believes and what difference it makes to his behavior. The world is full of Christian watchers. Stephen was known by the people of Jerusalem. There was nothing underhanded about him. He was a Christian — he knew it and they knew it. He was unafraid, and he was unashamed. He saw no cause to be defensive, so he went on the offensive. There was nothing apologetic about him so he took a dogmatic stand. Please note that when I use the words "offensive" and "dogmatic" I do so in the richest sense of the word. His was an attacking, virile, dynamic faith that was a constant challenge to all who knew him.

This was the opinion of the Christians in Jerusalem. They were called together by their leaders, and told to find an honest man, reliable and suitable for their purposes — a man whom everyone could trust. And immediately they chose Stephen.

The people in the pews knew him for what he was. I'm sure you have discovered that Christians are gifted people. The Bible talks about a diversity of gifts to be found among the Lord's people, but one that I have come across quite often is not listed as one of the gifts. It is the gift of criticism! Christians are people who seem to feel that they have a special dispensation and ability to be critics of all and sundry. Now I am fully aware of the fact that criticism can be invaluable, but I am thinking more of the destructive type that is not uncommon in companies of believers. Christians are experts at seeing flaws and discussing them at length. Particularly if the faults are to be seen in a person who has either been given, or has taken a position of prominence in the affairs of the church. No doubt the situation was the same in Stephen's time. In fact, there is no question that it was, for the appointment of the deacons came about because half the congregation was busy criticizing the other half! And vice versa of course! It was in the midst of this atmosphere that Stephen was recognized as a man of irreproachable character!

His character was not only vouched for by his Christian brothers, but also by his enemies. They hated him with a bitter hatred, but they respected him. Nowhere does the Bible give Christians grounds for expecting all men to love them, but I believe that the Christian ought to expect his life to instill respect into the hearts of the opponents of the Lord.

In the midst of his bookkeeping, Stephen found time for a preaching and witnessing ministry that was setting Jerusalem alight. Even the temple priests were getting converted by the score. Quite understandably the dignitaries of the synagogue got more than a little concerned. Stephen was hauled before the council and grilled by those bitter angry men. They argued and threatened, cajoled and blustered, all to no avail. Stephen was adamant and unshakeable. They tried to catch him with words, trip him with arguments. Still he held his ground. In desperation they bribed rogues to bring false evidence. They watched his reaction carefully, and they saw his face like an angel.

I'm not sure what an angel's face looks like, but I have an idea that there was a serenity about Stephen at that moment of tremendous pressure that made many a hard heart miss a beat! Even his enemies saw the reality of his life and were impressed. This is the caliber of a dangerous man. The devil gets shaky when he sees a man like this let loose and let go, for he knows the havoc that this type of man can cause wherever he goes.

It wasn't only his life that made an impression. His life certainly was irreproachable, but his works were irrefutable. Not only what he was constituted a challenge, but what he did also caused the devil problems. The sort of things that this penpushing deacon did are described for us in Scripture as "great wonders and miracles." Stephen was a man of energy, a man of action. He had the ability to make the sparks fly. I have no idea what sort of wonderful things he did. If God had wanted us to know, He would have told us. If He had said that Stephen raised a few dead people and healed half a dozen paralytics, that would have made us feel good. We would have said, "Good old Stephen. He lived in the age of miracles. Pity I don't, but there it is. I live in the day of small things. I can't expect anything much to happen these days."

It doesn't say anything about that kind of miracle, so there is no excuse for us. Wonderful things and miraculous things do happen today when dangerous men and women are let loose. Don't you think it is wonderful when broken families are reunited, when drunken men are made into responsible men? Isn't it thrilling when dope addicts are set free and give their lives to the service of their fellowmen? Isn't it a miracle when an adulterous wife is converted, and her life put in order? I am certain that Stephen saw this kind of miracle in his day whether he saw the more spectacular kind or not. These miracles happen today, and ought to be happening through your life.

The beauty of a life that is responsible for wonders and miracles is that it cannot be gainsaid. People can argue theology until the cows come home. They can discuss the psychological implications of mass evangelism ad infinitum. But there is little argument to be made about changed lives and salvaged homes, rescued families and new people. That is the value of a life that works wonders. It not only brings blessing, but it also silences the critics. Or if it doesn't silence them it means that they can only talk rot. Dangerous men do works that are ir-refutable.

There is one other thing about this dangerous man that I would like to mention. His words were important. In fact, his words were irresistible.

When his opponents gathered around him and asked awkward questions, Stephen answered them. When they were critical, he dealt with their criticisms. If they wanted to know something, he told them. But it wasn't only what he said that was impressive. It was the way he said it! There was something so compelling and dynamic about his words that according to Scripture even his bitterest foes couldn't "resist the wisdom and the spirit by which he spake."

As we have already seen, the defeated man has trouble with his talking as well as his walking. But Stephen, the dangerous man, undoubtedly had overcome this problem. When Stephen spoke, he did so with power and authority. This is the kind of talking that the men in the world appreciate. They are sick of mealy-mouthed ministers and double-talking politicians. They want something definite and something that rings true. They got it from Stephen in his day, and they deserve it from us in our day. I have discovered that, contrary to many opinions, unregenerate men welcome straight talk, and despise evasive talking. So many men are so unsure of themselves that they respect men who know what they believe, and can explain why they believe it. There is nothing to fear if you have something positive to say, and you say it positively. But there is much about which to be apprehensive if you have a message that you cannot or will not divulge. God will hold you responsible!

Please do not misunderstand me on this point. I am not suggesting for one moment that everyone will get in a line to kiss you when you speak like Stephen. Some of them, like Stephen's congregation, will line up to kill you. Yes, some will respond and the rest will react, but there will be no apathy if you speak like Stephen spoke. Let me remind you. The secret of his speaking wasn't his homiletic ability, or his oratorical polish. He was a businessman who preached in his spare time. He was a penpusher to earn his living, and a witness to fulfill his vocation. Stephen didn't say any old thing that came into his head. There was tremendous wisdom in his speaking. This is obvious if you read through the talk that he gave to the men who subsequently killed him.

It was an absolute masterpiece. He didn't have time to prepare it either! He was thrust into a situation where he had to speak right off the cuff, and what a great job he did. His talk was full of the Old Testament. He gave a brilliant exposition of the history of his people. There is no doubt about it, he knew his Bible. This is part of the problem today. Pew-sitters don't know their Bibles as they ought. You will never speak with authority if you don't tell people what God says in language that they understand. And you will never be able to do this if you don't know your Bible. There is no short-cut to knowing the Word of God. There are no twentieth-century methods of instant Bible knowledge. We have instant coffee and instant potatoes and, horror of horrors, instant tea! These are all devised to save time and energy, but there will never be an instant Bible-study method. You get your nose into the Book like Stephen, or you will never have anything irresistible to say.

This may sound as if he gave a first-class sermon. I've no doubt that he did, but it all depends what you mean by a sermon. I have heard sermons that were excellent in wisdom and outline, and they put everyone to sleep. I have heard testimonies that were honest and sincere, but as flat as pancakes. But there was something about Stephen's words that we must not miss. It was the spirit in which he spoke as well as the wisdom with which he spoke that made his words irresistible. There was a contagious enthusiasm and spontaneity that was a thrill to behold. I am sure it was thrilling to behold because it thrills me just to read about it!

Dangerous men believe what they believe so much that it shows on their faces. Their convictions are so real that they are delivered in such fresh, lively, natural tones that the listeners are caught up in the sheer exuberance of the message.

No doubt you have heard people speak with great wisdom and little spirit. On the other hand you have possibly met some full of spirit and sadly lacking in wisdom. The former speaker puts his listeners to sleep, while the latter annoys his listeners beyond words. Both are ineffective. Wisdom and spirit need to be married to make words irresistible.

Stephen was a great man. His life didn't take him to the top of any popularity poll on earth, but the Lord Jesus Himself stood to welcome him as he made his way to heaven. Who cares about popularity polls that are notoriously fickle when it is possible to be so dangerous for God on earth that the acclamation of heaven is a possibility. Better to live briefly and dangerously for God than to live at length and at ease for yourself. It is infinitely richer to be God's man on earth seeing

God at work, making inroads into enemy territory, than to be saved, but defeated. Are you dangerous?

Points to Ponder

1. Stephen's life was irreproachable.
2. Stephen's works were irrefutable.
3. Stephen's words were irresistible.
4. "Better to live briefly and dangerously for God than to live at length and at ease for yourself."

A Prayer to Pray

Lord, my life lacks impact. My works are very ordinary and my words are by no means irrefutable. Yet, I believe that You can use me as You used Stephen. Show me the secret of his effectiveness for the sake of my Lord and Saviour. Amen.

Chapter 11

Wherefore, brethren, look ye out among you seven men of honest report, full of the Holy Ghost and wisdom, whom we may appoint over this business.

But we will give ourselves continually to prayer, and to the ministry of the word.

And the saying pleased the whole multitude: and they chose . Stephen, a man full of faith and of the Holy Ghost, and Philip, and Prochorus, and Nicanor, and Timon, and Parmenas, and Nicolas a proselyte of Antioch:

Whom they set before the apostles: and when they had prayed, they laid their hands on them.

And the word of God increased; and the number of the disciples multiplied in Jerusalem greatly; and a great company of the priests were obedient to the faith.

And Stephen, full of faith and power, did great wonders and miracles among the people.

Acts 6:3-8

11

The Secret of a Dangerous Man

THERE IS A REASON FOR BEHAVIOR. THERE IS A SECRET OF EF-
fectiveness. Sometimes the reasons and secrets are hard to
discover, but on other occasions the secrets are so obvious that
they cannot strictly be called by that name. The life of Stephen
with all its power and blessing was so outstanding that he must
have had something to make him go, and if he is a picture of
the type of Christian so desperately needed today his secret
needs to be known.

His secret is one of those that is out in the open. If you
read again the description of this dangerous man looking particularly for the reason for his effectiveness, I think that you
will have no difficulty seeing what it was. In fact, it is so
obvious because a certain phrase is repeated more than once
in connection with his name. I am certain that the Spirit of
God led Doctor Luke to repeat himself in order that we might
have no possible chance of missing it.

"Stephen a man full of faith and the Holy Ghost." Then
notice, "Stephen, full of grace and power." It is also important
to see what kind of a man the apostles required to look after
the business, "Full of the Holy Ghost and wisdom." Do you
see the word "full" recurring?

Everyone is full of something. Some are full of themselves.
They are so impressed with themselves that they are almost
unbearable. People find them extremely tiresome because they
fail to see what it is that is so impressive. You have probably
met people who are full of problems, or the kind of people
who appear to be happy only when they are miserable. Some
have a consuming ambition and they are full of plans and ideas
revolving around themselves. It is certainly true to say that
everyone is full of something. Stephen was no exception. He
was full of the Holy Ghost and wisdom — full of the Holy Ghost
and faith — full of grace and power. Whatever fills a man

drives a man, and the thing that drives a man determines what he is and what he does and what he says. In short, the secret of a man is the fullness of a man.

One thing that the apostles said always shakes me. When they were looking for seven businessmen to be responsible for church administration they insisted first of all that anyone who was not filled with the Holy Ghost need not apply. In those days suitability for administrative posts in the church was determined by spiritual condition! Is that the case today? I fear not. Often the men who are responsible for the spiritual leadership of the church are not even examined on this point, let alone the administrative men. When you think about it, it isn't really surprising that we are losing our grip! It isn't hard to note the falling away of standards since those early, dynamic days. How can we possibly hope to make an impact on our day and age when we neglect the basic considerations of God's requirements? We are more concerned about education than spirituality. Popular preaching is more in demand than deep exposition of the Word of God. The men we elect to run the affairs of our churches are chosen for their business ability more than their spiritual integrity. By all means let us have businessmen for business positions in the church, and give us educated men for educated congregations, but don't let us mistake ability that is natural, for dynamic that is spiritual. Filled with the Holy Spirit first, highly qualified second — that is the correct order.

There are reasons for the reluctance of the twentieth-century church to think in terms of the fullness of the Holy Spirit. One reason is suspicion. "I've heard about the funny things that happen when these folks get all filled, and I said to my husband, I'm having nothing to do with it!" Or perhaps ignorance — "I can't understand the difference between the Holy Spirit and Jesus living in my heart. I get so confused that I have decided to leave it alone." Or believe it or not, denominational differences enter into the subject. "I'm an Episcopalian, and I don't want to have anything to do with this Pentecostalism!"

It must be said in no uncertain terms that there have been abuses and excesses in the name of the Holy Spirit. It cannot be stated strongly enough that there are those who are misleading the children of God on this subject. I want to say that any child of God who says "I am not getting involved in this doctrine of the Holy Spirit," is really saying, "I'm not going to get involved in God's kind of Christianity." It is as serious as that, for it is impossible for a child of God to live triumphantly and effectively in this day and age unless he does so under the dominion of the Lord and through the fullness of His Spirit.

I do not propose at this juncture to dive into any argument on this vital subject. Suffice to say that there is nothing to be afraid of concerning the fullness of the Spirit, save missing it! Instead I prefer very briefly to outline what is involved.

The first step to enjoying the fullness of the Spirit is to realize that you received Him when you were converted. When you talk about receiving Christ, you are saying the same thing as receiving the Holy Spirit. It is obvious that you could not possibly have received Christ physically into your body so the only possibility is that you received Him spiritually. The only way in which the Lord acts in a spiritual capacity is through His Spirit – the Holy Spirit. Therefore, to receive Christ spiritually, you invite the risen Lord to come into your life through the Holy Spirit.

The next step is to realize that it is possible to receive the Holy Spirit, but not to be filled with the Holy Spirit. The Christians at Ephesus who became Christians the same way that anyone becomes a Christian, by receiving Christ, were told to be filled with the Spirit whom they had already received. The reception of the Holy Spirit and the fullness of the Holy Spirit are not synonymous.

The third step is to note that Christians are commanded to be filled. This is not an optional extra for those who want "to go in for this sort of thing." It is a categorical requirement of God for His people if they are to live a life of value.

The fourth step is at first sight an elementary one, but nonetheless important. It is to realize who the Holy Spirit is. I am convinced that there is an appalling ignorance among Christians concerning the Holy Spirit. A few days ago a young Christian told me that she had discovered that the Holy Spirit was a person! But what kind of a person she still hadn't discovered. I wish we had more time to discuss this, but allow me to give you a golden rule concerning Him that will help you to appreciate what kind of a person the Holy Spirit really is. The golden rule that has helped me is, "Whenever God does anything big He does it through His Holy Spirit." Now I realize that having stated this dogmatically I must endeavor to substantiate. This will not be difficult.

In the first chapter of the Bible there is an account of something really big. God is creating the universe. The second verse states, . . . "and the Spirit of God moved upon the face of the waters." It is obvious that more than meaningless movement is meant here. The Spirit of God in some tremendous way was responsible for the mighty movements that were involved in the mighty work of creation. He was part of the dynamic of creation — that mighty force that is beyond our understanding. He is big, and He thinks big, and He moves big.

Then move on to another mighty happening in this world's history — the Incarnation. This is the event that brought the eternal Son of God to the womb of a virgin. When the girl Mary was told what was going to happen she apparently remained remarkably composed, but she did venture one perfectly legitimate question: "How is this going to work, seeing that I am a virgin?"

Now, bearing in mind the golden rule, we know the answer in advance. Listen to this: "The Holy Ghost shall come upon thee." Of course! How else would God work? For whenever He does anything big like creation or incarnation, He does it through the Holy Spirit.

Move on to another mighty event — the temptation of the Lord Jesus in the wilderness. You know the story, but have you noticed the important detail? "Jesus, full of the Holy Ghost . . . was led by the Spirit into the wilderness." He went into that mighty conflict with evil personified, in the power of the Spirit. Then He came out of the wilderness, and note carefully what the Scripture states, "Jesus returned in the power of the Spirit." Now, if the Holy Spirit was so anxious for us to know the condition of the Lord when He went in and when He came out, it would appear perfectly obvious that He wanted us to know that His condition was unchanged all through the shattering experience. He was filled with the Spirit. The dynamic of God in His life that enabled Him as a man to overthrow the might of Satan was the Holy Spirit.

Turn on in your thoughts to the next mighty event of this world's history — the crucifixion. Did you ever wonder where the Lord Jesus got the power to endure the physical agony and the spiritual suffering that He endured? Have you ever tried to think what it was that enabled Him to be made sin, and to willingly offer Himself as a sacrifice to God for sin? It was a chilling time, full of cruel passion and bitter hatred. There was the rejection of His people, the desertion of His friends, the estrangement of His Father, and the taunts of the crowd. Suffering and sin mingled with shame and spitting to make this event the all time low of human behavior. Those hours on the cross were the sink of human iniquity, and in the midst of it hung Jesus. How did He bear it? Listen! "Christ, through the Eternal Spirit offered himself without spot to God." The Spirit of God was the enabling force even on that "wondrous Cross."

But Jesus did not stay dead. On the third day He rose again — triumphant and glorious. He wasn't surprised to find Himself back on earth. He had been saying repeatedly that He would be back. His disciples didn't believe Him, but His enemies had their suspicions!

Think hard for a moment. Jesus was dead. His body lay in the tomb. The stone was at the entrance. The guard stood nearby. Jesus was in the realm of Paradise. He had been made sin, and He had sunk under the awful wrath of God. Defeat for the Crucified appeared a foregone conclusion. When suddenly the stone rolled away, the graveclothes rolled aside, the guards fell to the ground, and the mighty Son of God moved in irresistible power once again. Raised from the dead! How did He do it? "If the Spirit of him that raised up Christ from the dead. . . ." He, the Spirit of God, was in action on that mighty day, as He always has been in action when anything big is being done.

There is so much more to be said about who He is, but I feel if we can only grasp the immensity of His Person, and the possibilities of His fullness that will suffice for our purposes now. Have you seen that when you invited Christ to come into your life, He did it in the person of the Holy Spirit, who is always in business when God is doing something big? If so, we can proceed to the next step.

The actual meaning of fullness needs to be clarified. Many people seem to think that the Holy Spirit behaves rather like a liquid. The word "fullness" or the expression "filled" has quite understandably given rise to this mistake. You may even have heard that before a person can be filled with the Spirit, he must be emptied of self. It is in the same way that a cup that is full of water can only be filled with milk after the cup has been emptied. However, this is a slightly misleading analogy. The

Bible teaches that you will never be emptied of self. Your old sinful nature is with you for the rest of your days on earth. So if you are wanting to be emptied of self, you are wanting something that the Bible says you won't get. Further, if you feel that you can never be filled with the Spirit until you have banished self, you will have a long wait. Scripture teaches that the Spirit will wage a continuous battle in you with the flesh. It is obvious therefore that self will continue to be in evidence.

Don't get too excited, for this does not mean that you can indulge in self and be filled with the Spirit at the same time. Not at all! To be filled with the Spirit means that the self which is always with you is overpowered by the indwelling dynamic of the Spirit of God.

Remember that the Bible draws a parallel between being drunk and being filled with the Spirit. You may be like me, in that you have never been drunk, but you don't have to be drunk to know something about it. It is not necessary to be emptied of everything with a stomach pump in order to be filled with wine and therefore drunk. In my case, I would need very little to make me drunk. All I would need would be sufficient wine to overpower my faculties and I would be drunk.

This is the meaning of the fullness of the Spirit. It is His overpowering. Men are filled with the Spirit when they are prepared to abandon themselves to His dominion and to rejoice in His control.

The final step that I would like to mention here is the step of claiming His power and enabling and expecting Him to move in and through your life. You will appreciate that it is not uncommon to have a firm belief in the theoretical possibilities of the Lord working in your life without having any sense of anticipation that He will. Do you remember how Martha illustrated this at the tomb of her brother? Now we must underline the necessity of claiming the full empowering of the Spirit and expecting Him to start work through our lives.

Much has been written and said about the evidences of the fullness of the Spirit. There are those who believe that the only true evidence of this fullness is speaking in tongues and other signs. This, I believe, is not true, and I further believe that it can lead to great difficulties. On the other hand, there are those who hold an untenable position by stating that there is no such thing as speaking in tongues in this dispensation. My own coviction is that the unfailing evidence of the dynamic of the

Spirit of God must be demonstrated, not so much by supernatural signs, but by the fruit of the Spirit. In certain instances it may also be seen in the gifts of the Spirit. Signs are no substitute for fruit, but they may be an addition to fruit. Therefore major on the fruit and not the gifts. Get them in perspective and the Spirit of God Himself will protect you from abuse and excess.

There is no evidence that Stephen spoke in tongues, but there is great evidence that the Spirit of God got a wonderful grip on Stephen's tongue. It is quite possible that Stephen's miracles included healings, but there is no need to spend time surmising when there is so much evidence of the fruit of the Spirit in his life. The analogy of the drunken man helps here. A drunken man doesn't need to go around announcing that he is drunk. If he is drunk it will be obvious. I went to a wedding one day and a little man got drunk. He staggered in my direction with the greatest difficulty. As he drew level with me he lurched at an alarming angle. Then to my amazement he said to me, "I know what you're trying to do. You're trying to trip me up." He spoke with the thick slurred voice of a drunken man so that I had difficulty understanding what he was saying. Finally, when I heard him properly I assured him that I had no intention of tripping him up, and that in his condition if I breathed on him it would have been all that was required to put him on the floor. To my intense embarrassment he started to peel off his jacket and, swaying in the breeze, he adopted a stance that would have done credit to Cassius Clay. He was really in a bad state. You will see that his drunken condition affected him three ways — the way he walked, the way he talked, and the way he thought. A man filled with the Spirit demonstrates the same symptoms.

Stephen certainly did. His walk was so exemplary that everyone knew that he belonged to the Lord. His talking was so affected that his words were winged home in the power of the Spirit, and who can dispute the fact that his thinking was governed by the Spirit? When they murdered him, he died praying that the Lord would forgive his murderers!

Don't be afraid of being filled with the Spirit. Settle for nothing less than His mighty invasion of your whole being. He is your only hope. He is the secret of all spiritual effectiveness. Only when the Lord who died for you and rose again to live in you is allowed to rule over you through His Spirit will you know what it is to be dangerous.

Points to Ponder

1. Everyone is full of something.
2. Stephen was full of the Holy Ghost.
3. The Holy Spirit worked in the creation. (See Genesis 1:2.)
4. The Holy Spirit worked in the incarnation. (See Luke 1:35.)
5. The Holy Spirit worked in the temptation. (See Luke 4:1, 2, 14.)
6. The Holy Spirit worked in the crucifixion. (See Hebrews 9:14.)
7. The Holy Spirit worked in the resurrection. (See Romans 8:11.)

A Prayer to Pray

Dear Lord, now I am beginning to understand who the Holy Spirit is. I realize He is in me, and He wants to overpower me. This is what I want too. I now submit to your Lordship, and claim His fullness, and thank You for what you will do through me for Jesus' sake. Amen.

Chapter 12

And in those days, when the number of the disciples was multiplied, there arose a murmuring of the Grecians against the Hebrews, because their widows were neglected in the daily ministration.

Then the twelve called the multitude of the disciples unto them, and said, It is not reason that we should leave the word of God, and serve tables.

Wherefore, brethren, look ye out among you seven men of honest report, full of the Holy Ghost and wisdom, whom we may appoint over this business.

But we will give ourselves continually to prayer, and to the ministry of the word.

And the saying pleased the whole multitude: and they chose Stephen, a man full of faith and of the Holy Ghost, and Philip, and Prochorus, and Nicanor, and Timon, and Parmenas, and Nicolas a proselyte of Antioch:

Whom they set before the apostles: and when they had prayed, they laid their hands on them.

And the word of God increased; and the number of the disciples multiplied in Jerusalem greatly; and a great company of the priests were obedient to the faith.

Acts 6:1-7

12

The Caliber of a Dangerous Man

NEVER MAKE THE MISTAKE OF THINKING THAT THE FULLNESS OF the Holy Spirit is one blinding experience that sees you through the rest of your days. Almost invariably Christians come to an understanding and experience of abandoning themselves to His dynamic control through a crisis, but that is only the beginning. Crises develop into processes.

When Stephen was chosen by the Christians to be a deacon he was full of the Holy Spirit. Previously they had been looking for that kind of man, and they knew that he had been filled with the Spirit. Subsequently when he was murdered he looked steadfastly heavenward as the boulders shattered his body and he was full of the Holy Spirit. It is significant that the Scriptures are so careful to describe the condition of Stephen over a period of time. There is a serious misconception about the fullness of the Spirit. Many people seem to have gained the impression that the fullness of the Spirit is obtained in a blinding exhilarating supernatural experience so overwhelmingly dynamic that the recipient is never the same again.

This was not the case in Stephen's experience. No doubt he did have an initial experience when he intelligently, willingly abandoned himself body, soul and spirit to the Christ who through the Holy Spirit had taken up residence deep in the recesses of his being. Without question this experience would have far-reaching consequences. But there was more involved than a single experience. There had to be a continual step by step consciousness of the sufficiency and the all-powerful presence of the indwelling Spirit. More than that, there had to be a continual acknowledging of His sovereign Lordship and an unswerving dependence and reliance upon Him to control and to fill and flood his being. It was as necessary for Stephen to enjoy the fullness of the Spirit when he sat at his desk as when he worked his wonders. Stephen's remarkable composure and victory at the moment of his decease was directly the result of his abandonment to the Spirit of God. But Stephen didn't only need to be filled with the Spirit to die a martyr's death, he had also to be filled with the Spirit to live a Christian life. It is the continual fullness of the Spirit that is so important and so often tragically disregarded.

The old sinful nature was still very much alive in Stephen although you wouldn't think so. But the only reason you wouldn't think so was that the Spirit of God was being allowed to overpower this sin principle and continually deliver Stephen from the "law of sin and death." Even Stephen could have preached in the energy of the flesh. He could have resisted his enemies in the fury of mighty indignation at the way they were treating him. I have no doubt that Stephen had it in him even to have sunk to the depths of denying the Lord with oaths and curses when he saw that his life was in jeopardy. But he didn't, because at every moment that he knew the pressure of sin within him to react in the ways suggested above, he related this intolerable pressure to the controlling, mighty power of the Spirit of Him that raised up Christ from the dead. And He took over and demonstrated the power of His might through a body and a soul and a spirit that we call Stephen.

The relationship between the initial filling of the life of the risen Christ through the Holy Spirit and the subsequent continual filling can be illustrated from a common human experience.

Did you ever hear of a girl falling in love? I'm sure you have. When the girl fell in love she felt that her heart was full to overflowing, and that if she had any more love she would burst. But on the day of her marriage she had to admit that she loved her new husband more than she had ever loved him. Perhaps their marriage developed along certain lines, and they encountered all kinds of hardship and disappointment. This only served to deepen her love for her husband and when, after many wonderful years of marriage that had triumphed over trial and disappointment he fell seriously ill, she nursed him almost to the point of exhaustion. Never once did she complain. Not for a moment did she object, for her love was all-powerful, prepared to go to all lengths.

If on the day of her husband's death you were to ask her, "Do you love him more now than the day that you first fell in love?" I think I know what she would say. With a sad smile she would affirm, "When I first met him I thought that if I loved him any more, I would burst. But now as I look back I can see that what I thought was a love that couldn't increase in actual fact was nothing more than the beginnings of a love that has increased day by day."

The first day that a man opens his life to the Spirit of God in all His fullness he may be forgiven for thinking that he couldn't possibly ever know more of His presence and His sufficiency. But years of experience and days of all manner of trials and opportunities, victories and defeats, will only serve to deepen his capacity which the Spirit of God will be delighted to fill.

The dangerous man is never beyond the possibility of defeat. The Spirit-filled man will never be out of reach of the flesh, sin and self. There is no human being this side of eternity who can anticipate anything but conflict, for the more dangerous he becomes the more he can expect renewed attacks from the evil one.

During the war I lived close to one of Britain's biggest ship building yards. The largest aircraft carriers were built there, and one of the things that I enjoyed as a teenager was watching these massive vessels being built. The enemy knew all about them, of course, and was intent on destroying them before they ever put to sea. But he did a wise thing. When the ships were first started he ignored them. As time went by, and the aircraft carriers came nearer and nearer to completion, he showed more and more interest. Reconnaissance aircraft began to appear with increasing regularity. Then one night when we were all expecting it he came and bombed the almost completed ship. As night followed night the attacks increased in ferocity and intensity. It developed into a race. Would the ship sail first or would the bombs hit her and sink her? The longer the men worked on the ship the more dangerous she became. The more dangerous she became the more violent the attack. I am glad to say that every ship escaped fully complete and fully operative!

This is the picture. The more dangerous you become through an ever increasing fullness the more you can expect attack. As the attacks increase your vulnerability will increase. But in the degree in which your vulnerability is increased your dependence upon Him must increase. And He will not fail. He will overpower you and overshadow you in ever increasing fullness. I get worried when I hear people talking in glib, unthinking, silly language about victory in the Christian life. They seem to think that victory means vacation. Victory presupposes battle, not vacation.

Of course there is the other extreme. Some saints are so busy concentrating on the battles that they never win one through the power of the Spirit of God. The result is that they rapidly come to the conclusion that the Christian life is a battle and nothing more. The Christian life is a battle that you are expected to win. There will be no victory without a battle, but there need be no battle that ends in defeat. This was Stephen's experience. He lived a day by day, situation after situation experience of the fullness that God made available to him. Is it your experience?

The fullness that we have talked about leads inevitably to other things that we need to discover. Do you remember how we noted that Stephen was not only full of the Spirit but also full of wisdom, faith, grace and power? I believe that the fullness of these qualities comes as a result of the working of the indwelling Lord.

I have no doubt that Stephen was an intelligent man. But there is more than intelligence involved in what the Bible calls wisdom. It is not uncommon to come across highly intelligent men who are singularly lacking in wisdom. On the other hand, it is always a delight to meet men who are not particularly well-endowed with natural wisdom or intelligence who obviously have the touch of God on their lives and who demonstrate a deep grasp of the things of God.

Stephen was very conscious of the importance of this wisdom that enables man to come to grips with all that God intends a man to know and understand. It is interesting that he mentioned two men in his survey of the history of the children of Israel who were characterized by wisdom. He explained how God gave Joseph "favour and wisdom in the sight of Pharaoh." Joseph lived before the heathen king in such a remarkable way that even he had to admit that there was a divine quality about the young foreigner. Joseph's grasp of the essentials and the deep convictions that governed his behavior were so impressive to Pharaoh that even though he had no time for Joseph's God he had to acknowledge that Joseph's God was doing a good job on Joseph!

Moses was the other man who had wisdom but it was a different type of wisdom. He was without doubt a brilliant man, greatly endowed with natural intelligence, handsome and striking in his bearing. He was highly trained and deeply versed, but note, it was in the wisdom of the Egyptians. No doubt this wisdom sharpened his wits and equipped him for all manner of tasks. In all probability it taught him how to master the engineering difficulties inherent in building a pyramid. He probably had an advanced understanding of writing and literature. But it certainly did nothing toward equipping him in a deeper knowledge of his God or of preparing him to deal with the spiritual problems of the people he was destined to lead.

Perhaps if Moses had enjoyed more of the wisdom of God like Joseph and less of the wisdom of Egypt things might have been different. For instance, he would not have needed to ask God what His name was. He would not have refused to go where God sent him. He would have gone. He would not have bemoaned his own insufficiency, and would have rejoiced in the all-sufficiency of the great I AM. He would not have said his mouth couldn't give God's message. He would have relied on his God to give him the words to speak. The wisdom of this world is a great asset but it is no substitute for the wisdom that God gives through His Spirit.

As I mentioned in an earlier chapter Stephen clearly demonstrated a fine grasp of the Scriptures. The Spirit of God uses these Scriptures to impart to the child of God the wisdom of God. It is an exciting thing to realize that the same Holy Spirit who inspired the Scriptures takes up His abode in the heart of a Christian to interpret them.

What more could a child of God desire? Every born-again believer has available to him the One who was responsible for putting into writing the unknown mysteries of God! This means that every Christian has the golden opportunity of having a personal revelation and an intimate interpretation of the truth of God at any time. But, of course, he must first be in an attitude to the Word of God that will allow the Spirit of God to speak to his heart.

There is no doubt in my mind that there is a great dearth of spiritual insight and wisdom among Christians today because Christians will not dig into the Word for themselves.

A short time ago I gave a talk in California encouraging young people in a Bible College to make certain that they spent time in the Word of God every day. I tried to impress upon them that reading the Bible is not necessarily studying the Word of God. Many men read the Bible regularly, but they never study the Word because their approach to it is all wrong. Or they do not have the Spirit of God to make it make sense to them. Others go through a cursory daily ritual of reading a portion, but they never benefit because they do not allow the Spirit of God to speak to them through the Word. They are too busy to be still and meditate.

After I had given the talk a student came to me and accused me of being "unrealistic." She said, "How can you be so unrealistic as to suggest that we should spend time daily in the Word of God. We live busy lives, and it is impossible to give the time that you seem to think is necessary." I asked her if she ever ate food. She replied in the affirmative. "To feed your body?" I inquired. She nodded. I further asked how long she estimated that she spent daily feeding her body. She estimated approximately one hour every day. She admitted that her body would eventually die and return to the dust from which it had come, but she insisted that she ought to continue feeding it. But she had no answer when I asked her, "Why do you consider it unrealistic to take time to nourish your soul that will never pass away, when you find it necessary to feed your body for one hour every day, knowing full well that it will inevitably pass away?"

The only unrealistic thing about spending time daily in allowing the Spirit of God to impart wisdom to your soul through the written Word of God is failing to do it! And this is exactly what men and women are doing today. As a result they, like Moses, have a great grasp of the wisdom of the Egyptians and an ominous lack of the wisdom of God that Joseph and Stephen enjoyed and shared.

The wisdom that God gave Joseph, and which he shared with Pharaoh, affected the attitude of the Egyptian monarch. In the same way Stephen's wisdom had a great impact on the people of his time. Man in this enlightened twentieth century is confused because he knows how to get to the moon, but he doesn't know how to get to heaven. He has discovered how to make life, but he still doesn't know how to live his own life. He knows how to conquer space, but he still can't conquer sin. Modern man needs desperately a vision of the possibilities of God in his life and an understanding of the provisions of God for his life. The men who are intended to tell the good news fail if they are so busy with the wrong kind of wisdom that they, like Moses, have nothing of value to contribute to the thousands who would appreciate the opportunity to hear. This is the sad aspect of failing to appropriate the wisdom of God and the Spirit He longs to impart.

The second quality that I want you to notice is the fullness of faith that was evident in Stephen. It is quite clear from the way in which Stephen is described that his fullness of faith was linked with his experience of the Holy Spirit in his life. He was "full of faith and the Holy Ghost."

I feel that there are few more important topics for Christians than the topic of faith. The more I study the Word of God the more I am impressed by the fact that every aspect of the Christian life appears to operate on a principle of faith. Christian experience begins with salvation. We are "saved by grace through faith" (Ephesians 2:8). That being the beginning the Christian is expected to stand fast. We read that it is "by faith that we stand." This does not mean that the Christian is allowed to be stationary. "We walk by faith." But as a Christian walks he encounters all manner of problems which need cause him no lasting concern, for he can experience the "victory that overcometh . . . even our faith." When he needs advice from his Lord he has access through "the prayer of faith."

In fact, the whole of his experience is summarized in the oft repeated words of Scripture, "the just shall live by faith."

Now if a Christian is saved by faith and lives by faith, if he stands by faith and walks by faith, if he prays in faith and wins through faith, the importance of faith is plain to see.

Stephen was full of it! That means that every area of his life was enriched because of the caliber of his faith. There is so much to be said on this exciting subject, but I must limit myself to one or two basic considerations that may help the dangerous man to be more dangerous.

First, it is good to be reminded that everyone is full of faith. They wake up in the morning, look at the clock and believe. They switch on the light and expect it to work. They jump out of bed and trust the floorboards. They inhale deeply and never check what they are breathing. They stagger to the bathroom and turn on the tap assuming it will produce water and not sulphuric acid. And so on. Never a moment of a man's life is lived on any other principle than faith. This is necessary because man is so puny and dependent that he cannot operate without reliance and dependence on things and people all the time.

But, of course, the fullness of Stephen's was much more

than this normal fullness. Otherwise there would have been no necessity to comment on it. The object of Stephen's faith that was so implicit was the important aspect of his faith. The object of faith is always the most vital factor of faith. Some people have strong faith in weak ice. Nothing is at fault in their faith. It is absolutely full and implicit. Except, of course, the object! When the object of faith is wrong everything is wrong. We hardly need to be reminded that the object of Stephen's faith was the God who reigned supreme in heaven and who at the same time through the Holy Spirit reigned supreme in Stephen.

He trusted his Lord with everything. Even his dying words were words of glorious dependence and faith. "Lord Jesus receive my Spirit." In the hour of greatest battle his eyes were on heaven and his heart was at rest. In the time of his greatest agony he saw with the eyes of faith, "the Son of Man standing on the right hand of God." This faith was unshaken by attack and unmoved by circumstances. In fact, it persisted in growing stronger.

Faith in the right object always grows stronger. It invariably increases. That is why I have some difficulty understanding why people insist on asking God for more faith. If they were convinced of the possibilities of the indwelling Lord cutting loose in their lives because they allowed Him the right to cut loose, He would. Once a man has seen the Lord really cutting loose he is much more likely to try it again at the next opportunity.

This is a common enough facet of life. Have you ever seen a lady about to travel on a plane for the first time? She will hop from one foot to the other, chew her fingernails without even removing her gloves. When the announcement to board the aircraft is given she will dash to a seat by the emergency exit. The roar of the engines and the sickening feeling in the pit of the stomach as the plane leaves the ground will almost reduce her to hysteria. But notice the same lady six hours later. She is calm and relaxed — reading and chatting, smiling and eating. What has happened to her? Did God give her more faith? No! She started off with very little faith which she timidly placed with grave suspicion in the plane. As time wore on she realized that the plane was trustworthy. It didn't disintegrate. It didn't explode. So she relaxed a little more and then more and still more. The more she was convinced of the faithfulness of the plane the quicker she showed a fullness of faith that did the plane justice.

When a Christian has taken the Lord at His word and proved Him, he is much more likely to trust Him again more completely. If you have a weak faith it is because you haven't trusted the Lord with the faith that you have. If you had trusted Him you would have found Him trustworthy and more faith would automatically have developed. Over the time that Stephen had known the Lord this had been his experience. Nothing was exempt from this attitude of relaxed dependence. No time of the day or night was free from this relationship. Obviously he wasn't always conscious of this attitude, but it was so natural to him that if he had been awakened out of sleep by a crisis faith would have been his first reaction and the Lord would have filled his earliest thought.

There is no substitute for this kind of faith and it can be enjoyed by all who are prepared to live by it. This suggests that the will plays an important part in faith and this is perfectly true. You decide whether you will trust a person. You don't drift automatically into trust. In all probability you satisfy yourself that the person is worthy of trust before you trust them. So you see that the will decides whether you trust on the basis of the information that the intellect has amassed. Faith is not a nebulous indefinable entity. Faith is an intelligent act and attitude of the will that leads a person to trust and depend upon something or someone at a given moment.

If you have difficulties in this area check on your understanding of who the Lord is and what He promises to do and then find out if you are prepared to let Him do it. He will make of you a Stephen — full of the Holy Ghost — full of wisdom — full of faith.

Points to Ponder

1. "Never make the mistake of thinking that the fullness of the Holy Spirit is one blinding experience that sees you through the rest of your days."
2. "The dangerous man is never beyond the possibility of defeat."
3. "For by grace are ye saved through faith" (Ephesians 2:8).
4. "For by faith ye stand" (II Corinthians 1:24).

5. "For we walk by faith, not by sight" (II Corinthians 5:7).
6. "And this is the victory that overcometh the world, even our faith" (I John 5:4).
7. "But let him ask in faith, nothing wavering. For he that wavereth is like a wave of the sea driven with the wind and tossed" (James 1:6).
8. "But the just shall live by his faith" (Habakkuk 2:4).

A Prayer to Pray

Dear Lord, my Bible has been neglected, and my faith has been weak. I realize that through Your Holy Spirit You will work in these areas of my life, and I thank You for it. This I pray in Jesus' name. Amen.

Chapter 13

Ye stiffnecked and uncircumcised in heart and ears, ye do always resist the Holy Ghost: as your fathers did, so do ye.

Which of the prophets have not your fathers persecuted? and they have slain them which shewed before of the coming of the Just One; of whom ye have been now the betrayers and murderers:

Who have received the law by the disposition of angels, and have not kept it.

When they heard these things, they were cut to the heart, and they gnashed on him with their teeth.

But he, being full of the Holy Ghost, looked up stedfastly into heaven, and saw the glory of God, and Jesus standing on the right hand of God,

And said, Behold, I see the heavens opened, and the Son of man standing on the right hand of God.

Then they cried out with a loud voice, and stopped their ears, and ran upon him with one accord,

And cast him out of the city, and stoned him: and the witnesses laid down their clothes at a young man's feet, whose name was Saul.

And they stoned Stephen, calling upon God, and saying, Lord Jesus, receive my Spirit.

And he kneeled down, and cried with a loud voice, Lord, lay not this sin to their charge. And when he had said this, he fell asleep.

Acts 7:51-60

13

The Battles of a Dangerous Man

INTO BATTLE WENT STEPHEN, AS A FRONTLINE SOLDIER OF JESUS Christ. Mighty victories were won and much enemy territory was captured. Hearts in which sin had held control were flooded with light. Lives where the forces of evil had had it all their own way for years were captured by the Lord. Men who had been "led captive by the devil at his will" knew what it was to be set free from his tyranny. Even the stronghold of opposition to all that the Lord Jesus represented was stormed by these men of God, for a "great company of the priests were obedient unto the faith." Day after day the church moved like a mighty army crushing opposition, throwing down strongholds. They were thrilling and exciting days.

They were also costly days. No wonder that the forces who were suffering such major defeats began to hit back as hard as they could. The religious leaders were the first to react. They were seeing men who had gone along with their dead religion for years suddenly come to life. To their great dismay they saw an ever-increasing movement of men and women from their synagogues into the camp of the Christians. So great was their anger that they resorted to all manner of illegal practices. They stirred up riots. Even the law courts were abused by them. Men were bribed to give false evidence. Lies and blasphemies increased and anger and terror slowly and irresistibly began to rise. Then it overflowed and the church of Jesus Christ began to learn the hatred of man for the Gospel — Christians began to taste the sufferings of Christ.

Those early Christians were introduced to the shocking realities of what persecution can really mean. The words of the Lord about "taking up the cross" and "the servant is not greater than his master," and "blessed are they which are persecuted for righteousness sake," began to take on a new meaning. When He said that He was sending them forth, "as sheep in the midst of wolves," He hadn't been using high sounding challenges to which men would rise. He had been giving them a painfully accurate picture of what they could expect. No exhilarating hymns were needed to instill courage into those men. It was not necessary to use any noble catch phrases to get them moving. The battle was on, and those who belonged to the Lord were in up to their necks.

It is an awe-inspiring thing to be confronted with all the considerable fury of the forces of Satan fighting for survival. Strong men can be easily broken when the mighty forces of evil are aimed at them. But Stephen in the front line never wavered. He had an ability to stand firm under the most intense pressure. There was a capacity in him that enabled him to recognize all the subtle attacks of the evil one, for remember that the devil does not only use his crushing mighty strength, but on occasion he can be subtle and disarming.

I'm not sure when he is most lethal. You remember in Joseph's experience that on one occasion he attacked through the bitter brute behavior of his appalling brothers. There was an animal force about their attack that was not difficult to recognize and that accordingly could be met. When you know where your enemy is coming from you can face him and fight him, but if he comes from a new direction he needs careful identification and fresh methods of resistance are required. As far as Joseph was concerned, the devil followed up his crushing attack of brute force with the subtle soft disarming suggestions of a beautiful and wicked girl. I believe that there is not a man alive who is equal to the attacks of Satan, for this fallen angel of light is superior in power and intelligence to the highest man. He has at his disposal mighty armies of fallen beings, and under his thraldom live thousands of men and women ready to be mobilized at his command. What chance did Stephen have of surviving this sort of opposition? How could God possibly allow his child to be exposed to an enemy far his superior?

There is a simple answer, for in the same way that there isn't a man equal to the might of Satan there isn't a satanic power or personality equal to the dynamic of the risen Christ. This sounds rather comforting, but that is not all. The risen Christ by His Spirit in all His overcoming power lived in Stephen and lives in you. Stephen had all that he needed to stand against all that was thrown at him, simply because he had all that the Lord is living within Him.

Do you remember what Paul told Timothy? He said that the young Christian leader must be "strong in the grace that is in Christ Jesus." Do not make the mistake that many make when they assume that the only people who are strong in the battle are those who are born strong. If Timothy had been naturally strong there would have been no point in telling him to be strong. If he was strong he couldn't be anything but strong, and the command would have been irrelevant! The command to be strong came to Timothy and to Joshua and to Stephen because in themselves they were not strong. They were told to be "strong in the grace that is in Christ Jesus!" Now you will remember that Stephen was full of grace. He was simply an ordinary man who was full of the commodity that Christians are told to be full of and which they are expected to appropriate — the grace that is in Christ Jesus.

His grace is His goodness. It means His attitude toward us in being so loving and kind, so overwhelmingly forgiving and benevolent. It is only because of His grace that we live, move and have our being. If His grace did not exist we could never have known His peace. Through grace alone do we receive salvation and forgiveness, eternal life and assurance. Grace is at the core of all God's dealings with man. For, as we have already seen, all that man deserves is God's censure and disapproval. But the grace of God makes Him reach out to us in blessing upon blessing.

However, there is another special significance in this term. For grace is not only the attitude that makes God give. It is also the blessing that God gives as a result of His attitude. In other words, the grace of God in Christ Jesus means all the things that are made available to the person who is born again. The Bible has much to say on this subject but there is one verse that I feel summarizes the grace of God, "He is able to make all grace abound toward you; that ye always having all sufficiency in all things might abound to every good work." Isn't that a thrilling statement? Stephen believed it! As a result he was full of all that God makes available to His children through the indwelling Lord at any moment under any circumstances.

I am sure that Stephen needed vast resources of patience which probably he did not possess, but through the provision of the Life within him he was able to abound in patience. No doubt the things that were said about him by those professional liars who were bribed to testify against him, hurt him deeply.

He may have been tempted to hit back, but he knew a power of forgiveness within him that wasn't his at all. It was the working of the Spirit of God making the life of Christ real within him. He was full of grace, not his own, but the grace that is in Christ Jesus. Therefore Stephen could reckon on all that God had given him in Christ and use it! The patience of Christ was his so he appropriated it. The forgiving Spirit of Christ was his so he used it. Full of grace means full of all that it takes to meet all that the devil throws.

Imagine a soldier in the midst of a great battle. As the battle progressed his supplies of ammunition began to run low. Then his colleague was wounded and all his first-aid equipment had been used. At this critical moment the enemy staged a mighty offensive and it appeared all was lost, but, in the crucial moment, reinforcements arrived. The ammunition came through and medical help was made available. Not only that, the supplies never ran low again. There never was a moment when there was something that he needed in any of the thousands of situations that warfare brings, for he possessed in vast quantities all that he required. Stephen, "full of grace," was that soldier.

Stephen had all the resources of his base camp, heaven, within him. He was a frontline soldier with the adequacy of an unbeatable army. He was full of grace, and as a result the mighty forces of evil were unable to overcome him.

Of course, it is one thing to have the grace available and another to be full of it. You know as well as I that there are soldiers who hold an impregnable position, have all the ammunition and weapons they can use and yet they do not win a battle. The war in recent times between the Israelis and the Arabs illustrates this graphically. With numbers and resources on their side the Arabs were comprehensively routed by smaller ill-equipped forces. Why? Mainly because they did not have the will to use what they had and enjoy the victory that was theirs for the winning. There are Christians who are in a similar lamentable position. They appear to be totally incapable of winning a victory even though they have within them the One who has already defeated their enemy. The reason is that they fail to reckon with His sufficiency. They don't have the will to win!

When the pressure builds up they are beaten because they do not say "Lord, in your sufficiency I will not yield. Through all that You are I will claim the victory." This does not mean that the battle will be evaded. It means that the battle will be won. And there is all the difference in the world between the two!

Stephen did not get himself rescued from the hands of the howling mob on a magic carpet. He was left to the mercy of the gang. The battle raged on. But there is no doubt that he won that awful battle. This dangerous man was not only a specialist in defense; he was very much an offensive soldier, too. The grace that was his was for defense, but the fullness of power that was his was for offense. Stephen was not only "full of grace" — he was also "full of power."

No one will deny that the church of the twentieth century needs unlimited power if she is ever to make inroads into the vast areas of enemy territory. No pious cliches and orderly, well organized services are going to make an impact on the dens of iniquity that abound. Lovely services and beautiful music will fail to sweep demon-possessed men and women into the kingdom. Multitudes will not be added to the church as they were in Stephen's day by honest endeavor and ordinary procedure. More than this is needed. It will take superhuman power to achieve anything and the sooner we admit it the better for all concerned.

A few days ago a group of us decided that a large construction that had stood in the grounds of Capernwray Hall since the war ought to be removed. But it was made of solid concrete. Picks, hammers and chisels would make no impression. Honest sweat and bulging muscles were useless. The concrete could resist every attack upon it. Except one! Dynamite!

There is something virile about the words dynamite and dynamic. The very sound of the words suggest action, movement and irresistible power. *Dunamis* is the Greek word from which these words derive and in the New Testament "dunamis" is translated "power." This is what filled Stephen. He had a dynamic charge of dunamis in him! He was full of power. Stephen had what it took to crack solid resistance and blow it sky high. Make no mistake, it will take this kind of explosive to get the hard core of evil splintered with the Gospel in these days.

You may have been surprised to hear that we used dynamite to move our concrete slab. However, we obtained the necessary permission first. There was nothing illegal about our actions for we were fully authorized to act in that way.

The only people who are allowed to use dynamite in this country are those who have received the authority required, for dynamite in the wrong hands is lethal. Authority and power are closely related. Men who have authority without power make themselves spectacles and objects of derision. One day I saw a young policeman, full of authority and oozing with self-importance, try to arrest a large drunken man. The drunken man was too strong for him and without any effort at all deposited the young policeman in the gutter — authority and all. An older policeman came to his rescue. There was a calm authority about him that was a joy to behold, but there was power too. With a swift twist of his hips and a grip like iron he whipped the legs of the drunken man from under him. Then he pulled his jacket over his head, fastening his arms round his neck, and without a word, dragged him like a sack of potatoes, unceremoniously to the police station. The young policeman, looking decidedly crestfallen, followed at a respectful distance.

The two officers of the law had equal authority but one had the power to match his authority and the other had none.

When the Lord said "All power is given unto me in heaven and in earth," He used a different word for power — the word "exousia" meaning authority. Then He said that He would be with them. If all authority is His and He is with His people they have all His authority. It is the authority that is valid in heaven and on earth. Think for a moment. Stephen had the authority of heaven behind him because the Lord was with him, but he also had the dynamic of heaven upon him because the Spirit of God was within him. Remember that the Lord added, "You shall receive power after that the Holy Ghost is come upon you."

This is the position of strength for a Christian. He has the authority of heaven behind him and the dynamic of heaven within him. Stephen believed this and as a result was full of power.

When a man recognizes his rightful authority he is characterized by confidence. He doesn't have to go around trying to prove himself. It is obvious that the authority is his. If the man has the corresponding power he is a force to be reckoned with! That was Stephen, and that made him dangerous. Satan recognized his authority and hated it. He also felt the mighty impact of his power and resented it. That resulted in Stephen being a number one target.

Dangerous men don't only create danger, they attract it. The crack marksman on the field of battle will always be a prime target for the enemy. The star athlete on the football field always draws the heaviest tackling. The Christian, who like Stephen, rejoices in the all-sufficient power of the Spirit of God within him, draws the biggest temptations and the greatest opposition. That is why some Christians don't want to be dangerous. They prefer to be comfortable.

Listen Christian, we live in exciting days. There is much to be done and great victories to be won. Will you settle for anything other than the fullness of the grace of God in your life that will make you sufficient for all that comes your way? Are you interested in anything less than the dynamic of the Spirit of God in your life that will give the evil one plenty of headaches?

Let me repeat. You may have the authority of heaven behind you, the Spirit of God within you and the plan of God before you. Loosed and let go with all this power and authority you will be dangerous to the enemy, for God plans to deal him a body blow through you. The Lord intends to win victories through you. Can you, will you settle for anything less than dangerous Christianity?

Points to Ponder

1. "Blessed are they which are persecuted for righteousness' sake: for theirs is the kingdom of heaven" (Matthew 5:10).
2. "Verily, verily, I say unto you, The servant is not greater than his lord; neither he that is sent greater than he that sent him" (John 13:16).
3. "Behold, I send you forth as sheep in the midst of wolves: be ye therefore wise as serpents, and harmless as doves" (Matthew 10:16).
4. "Thou therefore, my son, be strong in the grace that is in Christ Jesus" (II Timothy 2:1).
5. "Have not I commanded thee? Be strong and of a good courage; be not afraid, neither be thou dismayed: for the Lord thy God is with thee whithersoever thou goest" (Joshua 1:9).
6. "And Jesus came and spake unto them, saying, All power is given unto me in heaven and in earth. Go ye therefore, and

teach all nations, baptizing them in the name of the Father, and of the Son, and of the Holy Ghost; Teaching them to observe all things whatsoever I have commanded you: and, lo, I am with you alway, even unto the end of the world. Amen." (Matthew 28:18-20).

7. "But ye shall receive power, after that the Holy Ghost is come upon you: and ye shall be witnesses unto me both in Jerusalem, and in all Judea, and in Samaria, and unto the uttermost part of the earth" (Acts 1:8).

8. "And God is able to make all grace abound toward you: that ye, always having all sufficiency in all things, may abound to every good work" (II Corinthians 9:8).

A Prayer to Pray

Dear Lord, I can see that there are battles ahead for which I am adequate only through Your grace. There are victories to be won that I will win only through Your power. Thank You for all that You are, and for all that You will continue to be. Keep me dangerous through the dynamite of Your indwelling Holy Spirit, in Jesus' holy name. Amen.